W9-BMF-302

Emilie Barnes

A Cup of Hope

HARVEST HOUSE PUBLISHERS
Eugene, Oregon 97402

Cover design by Garborg Design Works, Minneapolis, Minnesota

A CUP OF HOPE
Copyright © 2000 by Emilie Barnes and Anne Christian Buchanan
Published by Harvest House Publishers
Eugene, Oregon 97402

Library of Congress Cataloging-in-Publication Data

Barnes, Emilie.
    A cup of hope / Emilie Barnes with Anne Christian Buchanan.
        p. cm.
    ISBN 0-7369-0271-6
        1. Christian women—Religious life. 2. Hope—Religious aspects—Christianity.
        I. Buchanan, Anne Christian. II. Title.
    BV4527.B3585 2000
    242'.643—dc21

                                                                            00-039553

Contents

First to my family—my Bob, our grown Princess Jenny, our son Bradley, and all of our grandchildren: Christine, Chad, Bevan, Bradley Jae, and Weston. You continually bring me hope as I fight the battle of cancer.

Next, to all my friends, who have filled in all the gaps of my life. You have helped me, nursed me, cried with me, and supported me. The hope you bring cannot be measured.

Also—and with heartfelt gratitude—to all the women across the country who have prayed with me for more than two years. You have sent thousands of cards, shared hundreds of Scriptures, passed along so many messages of hope that keep me going. Many of you I've never met, but your love and encouragement have sustained me in hope.

Finally, to my very dear oncologist, Dr. Neil Barth, and all the staff in his office. You have ministered to me, caring for my heart as well as my body. You keep up my hope that I will survive this terrible disease.

In Christ there is always hope for today, tomorrow, and forever. I know that now more than ever before. To him and to you all, with a thankful heart, I dedicate this little volume of hope.

Emilie Barnes

1

A Sense of Tomorrow

*Y*ou know the old saying, "Where there's life, there's hope"? Well, I would put it a little differently. I'd say, "Without hope, life as we know it is simply impossible."

How can we survive without at least a tiny spark of possibility? How can we thrive without a healthy sense of promise? How can we grow unless hope keeps us looking and learning and moving forward?

That's what hope really is, after all. It's the desire and ability to move forward. It's a forward-looking attitude and a forward-moving orientation.

It's an interest and investment in tomorrow.

And oh, how we need that "tomorrow" orientation in our lives.

When "normal" life is spinning merrily along, we need that sense of possibility to keep the dailiness of home or office from wearing us down.

When life crashes and burns—when sickness strikes...or a pink slip arrives...or a friend lets us down...or we just seem to lose the way—we need hope as a lifeline to pull us through and keep us going toward better times.

In the past year or so, I've felt the need for hope more deeply than ever before.

During this time, I've come closer than ever before to understanding what losing a sense of tomorrow can do to a life.

You see, I've always been a positive, upbeat kind of person. I've weathered a lot of storms in my life with high hopes intact. But not even two years ago, I sat in an oncologist's office listening to a diagnosis that threatened to shatter all my hopes.

"I'd say you have a forty-to-sixty percent chance of survival," he said, "and that's *with a miracle*."

And then I felt the fear that can grab hold of hope and threaten to drag it under.

As I began treatment, with its side effects of weariness and nausea and pain, I saw more clearly than ever before how hope can diminish along with physical strength.

As I waited the outcomes of tests and underwent the seemingly endless steps in the journey of treatment, I realized how waiting and uncertainty can undermine even the strongest hope.

And as I lay open-eyed during long, painful, sleepless nights, I understood how hope can falter and flutter and seem to fail.

But I also discovered, in the midst of this difficult time, just how deep the wellsprings of hope are in the human soul—and what a persistent, resilient thing hope can be. For through this very difficult time of my life, I've actually grown more hopeful, not less.

The hope that resides deep inside you is stronger than you think. It's a survival mechanism built into you by the Master Designer. Even when it seems to be ebbing low, if you'll give it a chance, it will probably bubble back up again.

Think of all the improbable places in history where hope has managed to survive.

The Holocaust. The Civil War. The Black Death. Slave ships on the Atlantic. Atom bombs in the Pacific.

The Cross.

This last one is the most important, of course, for it's God's own answer to the question of what we can hope for. In the act of turning an instrument of torture into a symbol of redemption, he set the standard of hope for all of us.

Human hope, you see, is hard to kill—but it *can* be killed. It can run out of strength, or drain out into despair and depression.

That's why we need a hope that is bigger than we are to carry us where our human hope cannot survive.

We need a hope that is stronger than death.

In the past two years, I've tested the strength of a hope that prevails when human hope all but flickers out. In that sense, regardless of the final outcome of my cancer, I've experienced the miracle my doctor spoke of. For I've learned to lean on the hope of God the Father, God the Son, and God the Holy Spirit—to let myself be carried by the one who is the hope of the world.

And that hope holds, I promise you.

Even in the darkest, sleepless night, it will hold you.

Where there's hope, there's life.

A Hopeful Hint

A guaranteed hope producer is spending time with children. If you have some of your own, get down on the floor and talk to them; most important, listen to them. Let their youth and enthusiasm rub off on you and freshen your hope.

Words of Hope— and Hope from the Word

But now, Lord, what do I look for?
 My hope is in you.

—Psalm 39:7

But the eyes of the LORD are on those who fear him,
 on those whose hope is in his unfailing love,
To deliver them from death
 and keep them alive in famine.
We wait in hope for the LORD;
 he is our help and our shield.
In him our hearts rejoice,
 for we trust in his holy name.
May your unfailing love rest upon us, O LORD,
 even as we put our hope in you.

—Psalm 33:18-22

You, too, can find a place of silent power.
You can learn to see God in everything, to
listen for his silent language in your life....
Here on the wings of the wind God rides
into your life, whispering his presence,
Catching your attention. He brings to mind
other relationships that exist right now,
because relationships on earth remains
after the body is gone, even as the glow
remains in the sky after the sun goes down.
This silent language of love, this voice in the
wind, this undying presence is the unending
gift of God that permeates earth and out-
lasts time.

This language of love never dies.

—Don Osgood

I was just thinking one morning during meditation how much alike hope and baking powder are: quietly getting what is best in me to rise, awakening the hint of eternity within.

—Macrina Wiederkehr

Never fear, my friends.
The Center holds.
Whether we are centered or not, the
Center holds.

—Howard E. Butt Jr.

May the God of hope fill you with all joy and peace as you trust in him, so that you may over-flow with hope by the power of the Holy Spirit.

—Romans 15:13

2

There Is More

*J*ust what do I mean when I say I have hope—or that I want to find it?

The way I see it, hope is really several different things that go together.

For one thing, hope is a feeling. It's a sense of buoyant optimism, a sense that everything's going to be all right in the time to come. A feeling of hope is what puts a spring in your step as you step toward the future. It gives you energy and momentum, makes you want to accomplish a lot.

It's a wonderful thing to feel hopeful. We need that shot of energy that comes with hopeful emotions.

But...

The trouble with hopeful feelings, of course, is that they are fickle. Hormones can change them. The weather can affect them. They can be based on false beliefs and false realities. And they can abandon you.

If hope is just an emotion, you can't really depend on it. It's great to have, but you probably won't always have it.

So you need more than hopeful feelings to keep you going.

And there is more.

Hope, you see, is also a belief—an idea or conviction that life is eventually going to be better, either in the short run or the long run. Hopeful beliefs can be a powerful source of endurance and strength. Human beings can endure a lot if they believe there is hope for a better tomorrow.

But…

The trouble with hopeful beliefs is that different people believe *different*—and opposite—hopeful things. And they can't all be true!

Christians, of course, believe that Christ will come again at the end of history. We believe that there is life beyond the grave for those who trust in Christ. We believe that God is in charge of our circumstances and that those circumstances are working together for good. And our beliefs are obviously an important source of hope.

But some people believe that technology is the hope that will inevitably move the world toward a brighter future. Some believe that a certain social or economic program will make life better for everyone. The followers of the Heaven's Gate cult that made the news a few years back believed that if they committed suicide, a spaceship would come and take their souls to a better place.

Obviously, it's important to have beliefs that are not just hopeful, but also true. And they've got to be more than just ideas we hold in our heads, because human thought processes are notoriously fickle and unreliable.

Hope has to go deeper than the thought level if we're going to trust it. We need more than just belief if we're going to live with hope.

And there is more.

I have come to believe there is a hope that lives deep within the human soul—deeper than feelings, deeper than thought. It's a part of the way we were created, perhaps even a part of our DNA. History is full of stories of people who somehow managed to hold on to a stubborn hope long after they had stopped feeling hopeful, even after their conscious minds had stopped functioning well.

I think of Beck Weathers, the Texas physician who almost died during an expedition to Mt. Everest. Lost in a blizzard that killed the leader of his expedition, twice left for dead by his fellow climbers, Dr. Weathers somehow managed to get to his feet and stumble back down the mountain into camp. Some kind of hope buried deep inside him kept him putting one foot in front of the other.

I've discovered that kind of hope inside my own heart during the past few years, when I struggled with cancer. It's a will to live, a deep desire to go forward, that has grown stronger as my body grows weaker. It's a hope that's more persistent than emotion, more basic than belief. It's in my heart...and my bones and sinews and capillaries. It's powerful, and it's real.

But...

Even this deep, gut-level hope is not the most dependable source of hope, for it will eventually end in death. It will inevitably be tainted with evil, for that is the unfortunate fate of all good things on this fallen earth. And that is why our hopeful feelings, our hopeful impulses, even our hopeful beliefs, are not enough.

Our hope must go deeper than gut-level instinct, or it just isn't enough. There has to be more.

And there is more.

The good news is that such a deep, dependable hope is ours for the taking. It's more than a feeling or a thought or an impulse—though it affects the way we feel and the way we believe and the persons we are even at the cell level.

This hope is a person—the person of Jesus Christ.

It is his death and resurrection—and his living presence in our lives and our world— that makes hope the final answer to all the questions life can ask of us. Jesus is indeed the hope of the world—no ifs, ands, or buts.

So here, in a nutshell, is the hope that I pray you'll find:

- The *feeling* of hope—a positive emotion about the future.

- The *belief* of hope—the understanding that there is a worthwhile future to feel positive about.

- The *impulse* of hope—the stubborn need to move forward, even when hopeful feelings fade and hopeful beliefs appear doubtful.

- The *relationship* of hope—a restful, energizing connection with the one who is the Hope of the world.

≈

Without Christ, there will always be a "but" attached to my hope.
With Christ, hope always has the last word.

Words of Hope— and Hope from the Word

In his great mercy he has given us new birth into a living hope through the resurrection of Jesus Christ from the dead, and into an inheritance that can never perish, spoil or fade—kept in heaven for you.

—1 Peter 1:3-4

One truth about God which I continue to discover anew is that he has more for us than we can imagine. His plans far exceed our plans, and his grace makes possible so much more than we can envision.

—Nancy Pickering

Life with Christ is an endless hope, without him a hopeless end.

—Anonymous

3

Something to Look Forward To

$\mathcal{R}$emember the promises that adults used to make when you were little? If you behaved well and did what was asked, you were assured, something good would happen later.

Think about those hours you spent savoring the promises:

Tomorrow we'll go to the beach.

This weekend we'll go for ice cream.

If you help me mix the cake batter, you can lick the beaters.

When you finish cleaning your room, you can go outside and play.

Those promises were reason to hope! We lived in hope because we had something nice to look forward to.

And that's still true, every day, for us children of God. We have powerful reason to hope because God has made us a lot of wonderful promises. No matter what is happening in our lives in the moment, we still have a lot to look forward to.

Here are just a few of the things God has promised you in his Word:

• to delight in you (Isaiah 62:4; 65:18)

- to guide and direct you (Isaiah 42:16; John 16:13)

- to be your strength (Isaiah 41:10; 1 Corinthians 1:18)

- to limit the amount of pain and testing you undergo (Isaiah 46:9-10; Matthew 12:20; 1 Corinthians 10:13)

- to reward your faithfulness and good work (Galatians 6:7-9)

- to protect you in difficult times (Genesis 28:15; Isaiah 43:2; 45:1-2)

- to heal you when you are sick and broken (Jeremiah 30:17)

- to be with you and never leave you (Exodus 3:12; 1 Kings 11:38; Isaiah 41:10; 43:2; Hebrews 13:5)

- to eventually end your sorrow and bring you a wonderful future (Isaiah 35:10; 60:19; 65:19; Revelation 22:5)

- to hear your requests and give you what you need—and far more than you ever imagined (Psalm 17:6; Isaiah 65:24; Ephesians 2:20; Jude 1:2)

- to forgive your sins, take care of your guilt, and make good your mistakes (Luke 6:37; 1 John 1:9)

- to sustain you with whatever you need to live (2 Corinthians 9:8)

- to discipline you if you need it (Hebrews 12:6)

- to bring justice (Isaiah 28:17; 51:4-5; Ezekiel 34:16; Matthew 12:18)

- to send the Holy Spirit as a helper and comforter (John 14:16,26; 16:7; Acts 1:8)

- to make you fruitful (John 15:4-5)

- to transform you into something wonderful (2 Corinthians 3:18)

- to stabilize you when you wobble (1 Peter 5:10)

- to put you in a family if you're alone (Psalm 68:5-6)

- to be with you always (Matthew 28:20)

- to give you joy (Isaiah 55:12; Acts 14:17)

- to give you peace (John 14:27)

- to go ahead and prepare a place for you (John 14:2-3)

- to nurture and care for you (Jeremiah 40:4; 1 Peter 5:7)

- to help and protect you (Isaiah 41:13; 58:8)

- to bless you (Genesis 22:17; Haggai 2:19; Hebrews 6:14)

- to adopt you as his child (Romans 8:15; Ephesians 1:5)

- to include you in a kingdom that has no end (Daniel 2:44; Luke 1:33)

- to give you a future and a hope (Jeremiah 29:11)

- to give you something important to do (Ephesians 2:10)

- to make your burden light (Matthew 11:30)

- to give you rest and peace (Exodus 33:14; Matthew 11:28)

- to give you eternal life (John 3:16; 4:14; 5:24; 10:28; Romans 6:23; Titus 1:2)

Wow! That's quite a list. How can you help but be hopeful with all that to look forward to?

Of course, all these promises carry a big "if." They are almost all conditional—just as our parents' promises often were.

God will indeed do all these wonderful things...*if* we trust him, *if* we abide in him, *if* we give him what we are and let him live in us.

Now, these conditions aren't put on God's promises just to annoy us or make our lives more difficult. They're meant to prepare our hearts for receiving God's gifts, to make us able to live out the promises. The conditions are there because God loves us and wants us close to him.

And there's something else about all these promises. It was crucial to us as children, and it's still crucial to us today.

The thing is, promises don't mean anything at all unless you can trust the promiser! If our parents never took us to the beach or treated us to ice cream or let us lick the beaters, then we'd be foolish to trust them—and we probably would have given up hope long ago. Unfortunately, that is an experience some of us have to live through. People who make us promises are human. They're fallible. And sometimes they don't follow through on their promises.

But that's what's so special about the promises made by our heavenly Father.

He may not always work in the way we want him to, but he always keeps his promises. That's been my experience, anyway. When I'm obedient to him, when I pay attention to his "ifs," and when I'm willing to trust in his timetable, he has always come through. In my life, in fact, the only completely dependable promiser has been God the Father, God the Son, and God the Holy Spirit.

When he says something, you can believe it.

And that's why his promises ought to bring you a whole lot of hope.

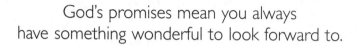

God's promises mean you always
have something wonderful to look forward to.

A Hopeful Hint

Photocopy the list of promises in this chapter and post them somewhere you'll see them every day—over the kitchen sink, on the bathroom mirror, next to your computer at work.

Words of Hope—
and Hope from
the Word

His divine power has given us everything we need for life and godliness through our knowledge of him who called us by his own glory and goodness. Through these he has given us his very great and precious promises, so that through them you may participate in the divine nature.

—2 Peter 1:3-4

We can so easily get in a rut. Our world can become humdrum. But let's dare to hope, to look forward to something, and let's don't feel guilty about it. It's a human need. Jesus told us not to be "anxious" about the future. I don't think he told us not to think about it or look forward to it. After all, he said he came to bring us the abundant life. Isn't that worth getting excited about and looking forward to?

—Bill Kinnaird

*I am with you and will watch over you wherever
you go, and I will bring you back to this land.
I will not leave you until I have done what I have
promised you.*

—Genesis 28:15

*Listen to me, my people;
  hear me, my nation:
The law will go out from me;
  my justice will become a light to the nations.
My righteousness draws near speedily,
  my salvation is on the way,
  and my arm will bring justice to the nations.*

—Isaiah 51:4-5

*I learned a long time ago that we as God's chil-
dren have no guarantees that we will not experience trouble. God never promised we would be
exempt from pain, but he did promise we would
never have to walk through the pain of this life
alone. He has promised he will never leave us or
forsake us, and we can depend on that.*

—Marilyn Heavilin

God is love, and God is faithful because he loves…he puts his love into promises to give our dull minds something to look at, and our unready hands something to hold.

—Alexander Raleigh

[We have] a faith and knowledge resting on the hope of eternal life, which God, who does not lie, promised before the beginning of time.

—Titus 1:2

If we are people of faith, we should remember the things that are important in the eyes of God, the surpassing concepts that should influence us. Whether we like it or not, longevity is not one of them. If we have faith in God's promises, we face life beyond our earthly years with equanimity, if not anticipation. Jesus has promised to prepare a place for us.

—President Jimmy Carter

Though the morning seems to linger
  O'er the hill-tops far away,
Yet the shadows bear the promise
  Of a brighter coming day.

—Frances Ellen Watkins Harper

4

Only Eighteen Inches

*D*id you know that at any moment of your life, you're only eighteen inches away from the hope you need?

It's absolutely true. I would stake my life on it. In fact, I *have* staked my life on it.

But it's also true that those eighteen inches may be the longest distance you'll ever travel.

Eighteen inches. That's the approximate distance from the top of your head to your heart. And that's the critical distance you have to travel in order to live with an enduring, unquenchable hope.

You see, you just can't live in your head and live in hope. There will always be too many questions, too many doubts. There's no real sustenance in intellectual belief. There's nothing to live on.

No, enduring hope has to reside in your heart—in the seat of all your emotions, your will, your connection with meaning.

But hope doesn't come when you live there in your heart alone.

Hope comes when you invite the God who made you, the Christ who redeemed you, the Spirit who surrounds you— when you invite the triune God to travel the same eighteen-inch journey from your head to your heart.

What gets you there?

You have to make a leap of faith, which is not easy. You have to weigh the evidence—the testimony of the Bible, the life experience of other people, and that still, small voice in your heart that keeps inviting you there. You have to pay attention to what is important. And then, at some point, you've simply got to take a deep breath and make that small and bottomless leap.

Now, I don't know whether this is a journey you've ever made. If you have, you know exactly what I'm talking about. You know that those eighteen inches can make the difference in terms of mended lives, mended marriages, mended relationships. It can make all the difference in a growing, enduring hope and a puny, pitiful hope.

If you haven't made the trip, though, let me talk to you from my own experience. I was once where you are. In my case, I was a Jewish teenager trying to decide whether the claims of Christ, which I had just encountered, were real. Whether the warm fellowship I observed in Christian churches and families was worth leaving my heritage in order to have. Whether the failings I observed in some Christians were enough to keep me from taking the journey.

Oh, it helped that I was in the process of falling in love with a fine, loving Christian man named Bob. But being in love was not a strong enough reason for making such an important journey. He was clear on that. I was clear on that. He would keep me company once I made the leap, but those first eighteen inches were mine to travel alone.

I did it. I said yes to the call of heart-deep hope, and yes to the hope of the world. And how glad I am I made that journey from a hope that lives in my head to a living hope that beats with my heart.

The interesting thing is that, after the initial leap, I've had to cover the same distance several times more. It was as if I had made a move and then had to travel back to pack up more and more of my life and move it to my destination. My thought patterns had to go along. So did my habits. My stubborn will sometimes had to be bullied to make the trip. My emotions had to be coaxed and cajoled. (Sometimes, even now, it seems like I'm always on the move from head to heart.)

And yet, after that first eighteen-inch leap, those other journeys were more like trips through familiar territory. They weren't always easy, but they didn't seem all that long.

For who counts the distance when you're hurrying home to Hope?

~

To find true hope, you have to go the distance between the head and the heart.

Words of Hope—
and Hope from
the Word

This is what faith really is: believing, not with the head or the lips or out of habit, but believing with one's whole life.

—Jürgen Moltmann

Trust in the LORD and do good;
  dwell in the land and enjoy safe pasture.
Delight yourself in the LORD
  and he will give you the desires of your heart.
Commit your way to the LORD;
  trust in him and he will do this.

—Psalm 37:3-5

Hope is not prognostication. It is an orientation of the spirit, an orientation of the heart; it transcends the world that is immediately experienced, and is anchored somewhere beyond its horizons.

—Vaclav Havel

How often had people heard that, for a Christian, death is but the ultimate triumph, a thing to celebrate? The hope was that it cease being a fact merely believed with the head, and become a fact to know with the heart, as he now knew it. He looked out to the congregation who packed the nave to bursting, and saw that they knew it too. They had caught the spark. A kind of warming fire ran through the place, kindled with excitement and wonder.

—Jan Karon, *These High Green Hills*

I will praise the LORD, who counsels me;
  even at night my heart instructs me.
I have set the LORD always before me.
  Because he is at my right hand,
  I will not be shaken.
Therefore my heart is glad and my tongue rejoices;
  my body also will rest secure,
  because you will not abandon me to the grave.

—Psalm 16:7-10

5

Love Is All Around

*Y*ou are loved.

You must take that to heart if you want to live in hope.

Remember that old song from the Mary Tyler Moore sit-com: "Love is all around"? I believe that really is true for you and for me.

Chances are, you are loved—imperfectly, of course—by at least one person on this earth.

Most likely you have been loved by others who are no longer living.

And it's an absolute certainty that you are loved deeply and passionately by the God who dreamed you up in the first place. You exist because God loved the world and loves you personally. As Karen Burton Mains once wrote: "You were made for the giving and receiving of love." Love is the reason you're here—to give it, to receive it, to understand it better. It's one of the main reasons you can live in hope.

The problem, of course, is *feeling* that love—really believing it, trusting it, taking it to heart so it can make a difference in your life.

Because we were created for love, it's all around us. Because we were redeemed by Jesus' sacrificial death and glorious resurrection, the love connection has been completed. All the love we could ever need is available to us right now. But because we still live in a fallen world, the loving connections that should bring us unquenchable hope can sometimes short out.

Some of us are loved by people who have difficulty expressing their love.

Some of us, for various reasons, have trouble receiving the love that is offered.

Human love gets warped by selfishness and anger and misunderstanding. And although God's love is perfect and always available, our own sin and the sin of others can block us off from the free flow of it. God doesn't stop loving us, but like naughty, confused children, we often pull away from his loving arms.

That's when we end up feeling unloved and unconnected, like bereft orphans instead of beloved children of the heavenly Father. Love is all around, but not, it seems, for us. And when we feel like that, hope begins to slip between our fingers.

Have you ever felt that way? Do you feel that way now, even a little bit? Then here are some things you can do to get back in touch with the powerful and eternal love that really is all around you, circling and enfolding you, every hour of every day.

• *Read the Bible with a pink highlighter pen in hand.* Underline verses that remind you about how much you are loved by God. (Use a concordance to help you.) Then go back every week or so and read your highlighted verses out loud.

- *Talk to God specifically about your difficulties in feeling love and ask him to help you.* Tell him how you feel, and ask for a sense of his loving arms around you. A counselor, therapist, or spiritual advisor might be his tool in doing this.

- *Take steps to mend a broken relationship.* Say "I'm sorry." Try to forgive a past hurt. Guilt and resentment can make it hard for you to receive the love that God and others have for you.

- *Make a point of hanging around with loving, giving people who are working to make the world better.* Love is contagious!

- *Say "thank you" to God and to others.* The attitude of gratitude tends to open your heart to love, and the act of expressing thanks to other people makes them feel more loving toward you. So cultivate the habit of heartfelt thanks. Learn to say "thank you" with smiling enthusiasm. Learn to write thank-you notes. Be sure your prayers are full of "thank yous" both for the good things in your life and the hard things God can use to teach you.

- *Practice delight.* Because he loves you, the Lord has put you into a beautiful world that can teach you and give you pleasure. The more you notice and delight in all this beauty, the more aware you will be of God's loving intentions toward you.

- *Show love to others.* The Golden Rule is psychologically valid. The more love you show to others through acts of thoughtfulness and kindness, the more love you will sense in your life.

- *Remind yourself that love doesn't die—that the love you have shared with those who are no longer here on this earth is still there for you.* Open your heart to memories of love.

- *Adopt a pet.* The act of caring for a dog or cat (or hamster or lizard) can increase your capacity to feel and express love.

- *Learn to nurture yourself.* Feeling uncared for can harden your heart with resentment and feelings of unworthiness. So you can actually increase your capacity to love and be loved by taking better care of yourself—eating right, exercising regularly, surrounding yourself with beauty, enjoying fun things.

~

Your hope will grow as you become
more aware of the love
that is all around you.

Words of Hope—
and Hope from
the Word

God is like a blanket always ready to be
  wrapped around you.
God is like a chair always there to hold you.
God is like a pair of arms always ready to wrap
  you in a hug.
God is like anything you can thing of, only much
  better and sweeter.

—Suzie Godfrew
(written in a loving card sent to me)

I will not leave you as orphans; I will come to you.

—John 14:18

Love is as strong as death....
Many waters cannot quench love;
rivers cannot wash it away.

—Song of Songs 8:6-7

Dear friends, let us love one another, for love comes from God. Everyone who loves has been born of God and knows God....No one has ever seen God; but if we love one another, God lives in us and his love is made complete in us....And so we know and rely on the love God has for us. God is love. Whoever lives in love lives in God, and God in him. In this way, love is made complete among us.

—1 John 4:7-12, 16-17

Can a woman forget her nursing child and have no compassion on the son of her womb? Even these may forget, but I will not forget you. Behold, I have inscribed you on the palms of my hands.

—Isaiah 49:15-16 NASB

You have to read that beautiful passage in Isaiah where God speaks and says: "I have called you by name. You are mine. Water will not drown you, fire will not burn you. I will give up nations for you. You are precious to me."

We are precious to him. That man dying in the street—precious to him. That millionaire—precious to him. That sinner—precious to him. Because he loves us.

—Mother Teresa of Calcutta

At this moment somebody is
very proud of you. Somebody is thinking
of you, somebody misses you. Somebody trusts you. Somebody is caring about you. Somebody wants to talk to you. Somebody
hopes you are not in trouble. Somebody is thankful for the support you have
provided. Somebody wants to hold your hand. Somebody hopes everything turns
out all right. Somebody wants you to be happy. Somebody wants to hug you.
Somebody thinks you are a gift. Somebody admires your strength. Somebody
wants to protect you. Somebody is thinking of you and smiling. Somebody
can't wait to see you. Somebody loves you for who you are. Somebody
treasures your spirit. Somebody needs your encouragement. Somebody is glad that you are their friend. Somebody wants to
get to know you better. Somebody wants you to
know they are there for you. Somebody would
do anything for you. Somebody wants
to share their dreams with you.
Somebody needs your
support. Somebody
loves
you.

—from a card I received

40

6

Faith for the Climb

*Y*ou just can't see as much when you're climbing the mountain as you can from the top.

I guess that's obvious if you're hiking in the Rockies or the Smokies or the Himalayas. But it's not always so evident when you're just trying to get through life.

Sometimes it's hard to know where your life is going. From where you are, on the side of the mountain, you might not even see the summit. The winding trail might not seem to be going anywhere. Sometimes it might even seem to go downhill!

Sometimes it's hard to tell which of two tempting directions is the best to take. Is it better to take the meandering trail or the steep climb over the rocks? Should you push on harder to reach the top? Should you rest and take your time and risk bad weather later on?

And sometimes you get so confused and discouraged and downright weary, you're tempted to just give up hope altogether.

But it helps to keep in mind exactly what's going on.

You're climbing a mountain, remember, and one day you'll reach the top. One day you'll be able to stand and look out over all the valleys—even look back at the winding path that brought you to the top—and it will all become clear.

I try to think of that on the days when I'm fatigued or in pain or just discouraged, when I'm confused and worried about what will happen to me next.

I'm still on the mountain, so I've got to remember that my perspective is faulty. I just don't have the whole picture the way God does, the way I will have it someday.

Oh, I have some pretty good hints. I have instructions from the One who created the mountain. I have stories from climbers who have gone on the path before me and companions who are climbing with me. (How I depend on their help and encouragement!) And of course I have those moments along the way when wonderful vistas suddenly unfold before me, when I round a corner to see the checkered valleys spread out below and the summit shining whitely up above.

I have all that to enable me as I climb up this mountain called Life. You do, too. I really believe that the God who created us and redeemed us has equipped us with what we need to make it to the top.

Still, we have to face the fact that some of the time, maybe most of the time, we won't be able to see exactly where we're going.

But that's where faith comes in. Faith always travels hand in hand with hope—it's what enables us to keep our hopes up when the way becomes rockier and more obscure. Faith is what we need to keep moving on, moving up, trusting our Guide, trusting it will all be worth it.

Trusting that if we continue on, we'll make it to the top and everything will be all clear.

And yes, I know that's hard to remember when you're stuck on the mountainside. But it might help to follow this brief checklist for keeping up your hopes while you're climbing hard or when you think you might be lost:

- *Trust the climbing map*—God's Word—and pay attention to your Guide. You're not expected to make this climb without help.

- *Pace yourself*—you don't have to make it all in one day. Without adequate rest, you'll never make it to the summit.

- *Remember where you are and where you're going*—but try to accept that your perspective is limited. (That's why you have the map and the Guide!)

- *Refresh yourself by remembering the goal*—and those moments when it was all clear to you.

- *Look back to where you've been* and be grateful for your progress.

- *Help and enjoy your fellow climbers.*

- *Take care of your equipment*—your body, mind, and spirit. They've been issued to you by God, and they'll help carry you to where you need to be.

Only God has the big picture for where you're going, but he's given you what you need to journey successfully.

Words of Hope— and Hope from the Word

Hope is the feeling we have that the feeling we have is not permanent.

—Mignon McLaughlin

So we are always confident, knowing that while we are at home in the body we are absent from the Lord. For we walk by faith, not by sight.

—2 Corinthians 5:6-7 NKJV

Eternity is the divine treasure house, and hope is the window, by means of which mortals are permitted to see, as through a glass darkly, the things which God is preparing.

—William Mountford

Our life is like a tapestry of intricate design
With lovely patterns taking shape as colors
  intertwine,
Some of the threads we weave ourselves
By things we choose to do—
Sometimes a loving Father's touch adds a special
  hue.
And though tomorrow's pattern is not for us to
  see—
We can trust his faithful hand through all eternity.

—Author unknown

You have made known to me the path of life;
  you will fill me with joy in your presence,
  with eternal pleasures at your right hand.

—Psalm 16:11

We need hope for living, far more than for dying. Dying is easy work, compared to living. Dying is a moment's transition; living, a transaction of years. It is the length of the rope that puts the sag in it. Hope tightens the words and tunes up the heartstrings.

—Telescope

To travel hopefully is a better thing than to arrive.

—Robert Louis Stevenson

7

A Nibble of Hope

*H*ave you ever noticed that it's often the little things in life that drag you down?

I'm talking about the small annoyances, the petty pains, the everyday griefs that combine to pull at your spirit and nibble away at your hope.

The little quarrel with your sister and the sarcastic remark from your husband.

The little pile of junk in the corner you never quite get around to cleaning out.

The little aches and pains that don't seem quite serious enough to take to a doctor.

The little twinge of guilt over something you meant to do or disappointment over something you wanted but couldn't get.

Artist Thomas Kinkade calls them the "nibblers"—because they are often the little things that "eat away at your happiness and steal your joy." I really like that term *nibblers*, because that's what it feels like when I let the little things get to me.

They can also, if you let them, do a number on your capacity to hope.

In fact, I think it's far more common for hope to be dribbled and nibbled away by a bunch of little worries than for it to be destroyed in one fell swoop. It's like being devoured by piranhas! One worry starts eating at you, then another, then it's joined by some feelings of guilt or shame, and then here's a little problem you can't solve...and pretty soon you realize your heart is more full of quiet desperation than shining hope.

How do you fight these little marauders? I have found two different strategies to be helpful.

First of all, you fight the nibblers by remembering what they are. They're small. They're really not important—unless you let them be. And each one by itself is not hard to handle— if you need to handle it at all. Some nibblers, I have found, are really little lies. They claim to be problems that need our attention, but they're not really issues we can do anything about. The more we let them eat at us, the more our desperation can grow.

So the first thing to do in fighting the nibblers is to take them one at a time and either solve them or let them go. Tell your sister you're sorry. Make up with your husband. Take fifteen minutes and clean up the corner. Take an aspirin or make an appointment with the doctor. Pray about the disappointment. Either act on the guilt or face it and tell it to go away.

And in the meantime, while you're dealing with the nibblers on a one-to-one basis, consider some positive things you can do to counter the attacks of the nibblers.

After all, if little things can drag you down, little things can also pick you up. So the second way you can fight the nibblers and build up hope is to develop an arsenal of *little* hope builders that bolster your spirits and remind you of your possibilities.

Your list might be different from mine, but here are some ideas:

- *Keep something green* in a little vase or pot over your kitchen sink.

- *Find a small gift book that lifts your spirits and gives you hope*—prayers, affirmations, Scripture verses, or even just pretty pictures. Leave it in a shelf or basket in your bathroom as a little source of hope during those "necessary" moments when you are alone.

- *Schedule a lunch break or an afternoon tea* out with an encouraging friend.

- *Spend an occasional lunch hour rocking newborns* in a hospital nursery or volunteering at a daycare center.

- *Write some favorite Scripture promises* on sticky notes and post them on your bathroom mirror, on the TV screen, or even in your underwear drawer.

- *Find a lovely place where you can walk to boost your spirits*—a park, an arboretum, a beautifully landscaped mall. Try to walk there at least once a week.

- *Put together a little collection of things that mean hope to you*—pictures of your family, pebbles from a beach, a hank of kite string, a tulip bulb, a miniature cross or Easter egg. Keep your collection in a little box—your very own "hope chest"—or hot glue it onto a poster or arrange it on a table to remind you of all you have to hope for.

∾

Little things can mean a lot
when it comes to keeping hope in your life.

Words of Hope—
and Hope from
the Word

Catch for us the foxes, the little foxes that ruin the vineyards, our vineyards that are in bloom.

—Song of Songs 2:15

Everything that is done in the world is done by hope. No husbandman would sow one grain of corn if he hoped not it would grow up and become seed; no bachelor would marry a wife if he hoped not to have children; no merchant or tradesman would set himself to work if he did not hope to reap benefit thereby.

—Martin Luther

Lay hold upon the hope set before us: which hope we have as an anchor of the soul, both sure and stedfast.

—Hebrews 6:18-19 KJV

How do you fight the [nibblers]? Nine times out of ten, I've found, you can do it by telling the truth!

That's because nibblers are really liars. They like to plague us with problems that aren't really problems, situations we've already taken care of, circumstances we can't do anything about. So I have found the best way to counter their fibs and prevarications is simply to call their bluff…

Occasionally, of course, I will realize that a nibbler or a set of nibblers derives from a situation that really does require some action on my part. In cases like that, I can still answer them no by making a specific plan: "No, that's not going to be a problem because I'm going to do this to take care of it."

Saying no to the nibblers, in other words, is simply a matter of facing reality. The truth is that worrying about problems…will never do anything but drain your heart of its joyful color.

—Thomas Kinkade, *Lightposts for Living*

8

Clean and New

*H*ave you ever come in from traveling or working outdoors and felt really dirty? You know what I mean—that sticky, uncomfortable feeling, as if a layer of grime were coating you from head to toe. Your head itches. Your teeth feel coated. You smell sweaty. And although there's a lot that you need to be doing, you just can't concentrate on doing anything until you get clean.

So you come inside and shed those dirty clothes and step into a hot shower. It might be a little hotter than is comfortable at first, but soon it feels wonderful! You scrub and soap and rinse until your skin is all rosy and your hair is squeaky clean. Then you step out onto a fluffy bath mat, grab a big thirsty towel to dry off, dry your hair, and fix your face and then you're ready for the world. You feel like a new person—ready to tackle any new task that comes along.

Well, to me, that hot, soapy shower is a great parable of the way hope comes from forgiveness and reconciliation. Living in this world, we can't help but accumulate a coating of guilt and shame and anger and resentment. People we love hurt us. We hurt others. Little tiffs grow into big estrangements. And pretty soon, unless we do something about it, we find that we're feeling discouraged and dirty instead of positive and hopeful.

If you're a Christian, you already know that repentance and forgiveness are important. We need to confess our sins and repent and seek the Father's forgiveness on a daily basis. We need to be willing to extend forgiveness to others. We need to do all that to keep our relationship to Christ alive.

But here's another reason we need to keep our hearts clean. It's because a clean heart is a hopeful heart. It's very hard for us to keep moving forward into the possibilities of the future when we're covered with the grime of past sins—our own or others.

I learned that lesson anew during the very difficult time when our daughter Jenny left her first husband. That was a time when I was sure my heart would break—especially for Jenny's three children, our precious grandchildren, but also for our daughter and our son-in-law, whom we dearly loved. And though I tried very hard to be supportive and loving, there was still a part of me that blamed Jenny for making things hard on all of us.

I wasn't really aware of that, though. All I knew clearly was that the situation needed a lot of prayer. So I prayed and prayed and prayed—combining prayers for Jenny with my daily exercise walks. I prayed that she would come to her senses and go back to her husband. I prayed that she would become the strong woman of God she was created to be. I prayed that there would be healing in our family.

And for the longest time, none of that seemed likely to happen. What a long time of painful waiting that was! And there were times, I have to confess, that I almost fell into despair. Nothing seemed to get better. There was no reconciliation. My grandchildren were hurting. My Bob was angry and frustrated. My stress was showing itself in physical symptoms.

And then God did a surprising thing. Instead of simply granting what I asked, God gave me a look inside myself. And what I saw was a layer of dirt and grime on my heart I hadn't even known was there. Though I was praying for Jenny, helping her whenever I could, and trying to keep from preaching at her or telling her what to do, in my heart I was nurturing anger and bitterness and unforgiveness toward her.

And what was I supposed to do with my grime-encrusted heart? The Holy Spirit was clear as it whispered the next step.

Go to Jenny, the familiar voice whispered in my spirit, *and ask her forgiveness.*

Well, you can guess how that went over with me! Why was I the one who had to ask forgiveness? *She* was the one in the wrong.

If there's one thing I've learned, though, in my years of being a Christian, it's that saying no to God gets us in a lot of trouble. So I did go to Jenny. I confessed my bitter feelings toward her and asked forgiveness. I asked God's forgiveness, too. I repented of my hard attitudes and came clean.

And do you know the most important thing that came out of that time together?

Hope.

I began to have the sense that God was at work, though nothing changed immediately. I began to be aware that the healing would come—and it has, although not in the way I would have scripted it.

From that moment when I went to Jenny and began to scrub the grime off my heart, I began to feel the freedom of hope.

If you're feeling discouraged right now, that's something you might want to think about. If your hope is draining low, there's a good chance that you've let some grime accumulate on the surface of your heart.

The "how to" of coming clean is clearly outlined in the Bible. You ask God to show you where you are unclean. You repent of your sins, confess them to God, and ask forgiveness. You ask for his help in reconciling with other people—both asking forgiveness and forgiving others.

Sometimes the whole process will be a little uncomfortable. Hot water and scrubbing doesn't always feel good, especially if the dirt has been around awhile. (Like any cleansing process, it's easier if it happens every day!)

But remember that wonderful clean feeling you get as a result? Remember the sense that you're finally ready for anything?

It's the way we're meant to live.

Rosy, clean...and full of hope.

~

Hope comes from repentance,
forgiveness, and reconciliation.

Words of Hope— and Hope from the Word

Repentance is not necessarily the gloomy and self-loathing practice it is sometimes made out to be. To repent is not to be confirmed in what that little voice within keeps whispering: that you are no good, that everything bad that happens to you is your own fault, that if only others knew what you were really like, they would cease to care for or be interested in you. No. True repentance begins with the felt knowledge that we are loved by God. We are children of God. If we cannot find ourselves there then perhaps our preparation might consist of the prayer that we might know ourselves as beloved, that the divine lover might reach down into our self-hatred…and touch us.

—Wendy M. Wright

Have mercy on me, O God,
  according to your unfailing love;
according to your great compassion
  blot out my transgressions.
Wash away all my iniquity
  and cleanse me from my sin....
Surely you desire truth in the inner parts;
  you teach me wisdom in the inmost place.
Cleanse me with hyssop, and I will be clean;
  wash me, and I will be whiter than snow.
Let me hear joy and gladness;
  let the bones you have crushed rejoice....
Create in me a pure heart, O God,
  and renew a steadfast spirit within me.
Do not cast me from your presence
  or take your Holy Spirit from me.
Restore to me the joy of your salvation
  and grant me a willing spirit, to sustain me.
Then will I teach transgressors your ways,
  and sinners will turn back to you.

—Psalm 51:1-2,6-8,10-13

So shall the world be created each morning
anew, forgiven—in thee, by thee.

—Dag Hammarskjöld

9

When to Give Up Hope

One of the most important ways I've found to keep hope in life is to let God be God.

And yes, that makes more sense than it sounds like at first!

You see, I think that sometimes we miss out on the hope that God has for us because we insist on finding it where we want to find it—in the form that we want to find it—instead of opening our minds and our hearts to receive it as God wants to give it.

Maybe we consciously set our hearts and our hopes on a happy, fruitful marriage...or a child...or a successful career...or an interesting life in a certain geographical area. Or maybe we just assume that our life will include certain amenities like good health or a happy family or a comfortable income. Then, if those wishes and assumptions are not fulfilled, we may find ourselves feeling disappointed and discouraged and even abandoned by God instead of joyful and hopeful and rejoicing in his presence.

We've gotten our hopes up, and we feel let down because life hasn't turned out the way we wanted. And as we mope about with our eyes cast down, we may find it hard to grasp the signs of new hope that are all around us.

How easy it is to miss out on hope when we forget who's in charge of the universe—and in charge of all we can hope for!

This has been a poignant lesson for me in the past few years. Again and again I've had to learn this lesson of letting God be God even in regard to my fondest hopes and dreams.

For a long time, for instance, I placed all my hopes in seeing my daughter's marriage restored. And it didn't happen. But when I finally got my heart around to letting God be God, I began to receive the gifts of hope he was waiting to give me— the gift of watching my daughter grow as a mature woman of God, of watching our relationship flourish and deepen, and of seeing the circumstances of her life blossom as she chose to repent and be obedient to him.

More recently, I placed all my hopes on regaining my health—on feeling wonderful again. But gradually I've come to the point of letting go of those hopes, too. Oh, I'm still trusting in God to heal me! But I'm coming to the point where I have to let God be God in this area, too, and not dictate to him how my hopes are to be fulfilled.

If I insisted on feeling good in order to feel hopeful—well, there would be many days when my cup of hope turned up empty! If I insisted on a positive blood report, my hopes would fluctuate with every visit to my doctor.

But I've learned that if I can wait and keep my heart and mind open, hope comes to me in surprising ways. Not necessarily in the form of feeling good or receiving a positive health report, but in a variety of wonderful ways: in a visit from my grandchildren. In the beautiful gift of a friend who will crawl up on the bed and weep with me. In the words of a card that wrap me in a cocoon of caring or a remembered Scripture verse that reminds me of God's promises.

In those small gifts of hope, I find the energy and will to keep going. I find the support and encouragement I need to wait patiently for the larger fulfillment of my hopes. They might not be exactly what I thought I wanted, but somehow they connect me more closely to God than getting my own way would.

So here's what I'm trying to keep in mind throughout this difficult chapter of my life: God is God—and let him be God!

He's not a servant at my beck and call, programmed to bring me what I want when I want it. Instead, he's a loving Father who loves me and loves to surprise me.

Yes, he has promised to give me a future and a hope. If I trust his Word, the gifts he has in store for me will be unimaginably wonderful. There will be comfort and stability and dancing and feasting. His goal for me is nothing less than the inheritance of his kingdom.

But today and tomorrow, he's going to do it his way. And sometimes that means I almost have to give up hope in order to find hope. I have to let go of my right to have things just the way I want them, just the way I hope for, and trust him for my hope the same way I trust him for my daily bread.

But if I'm willing to accept those terms and wait for him, the hope he brings me is always enough.

Even better, it's a wonderful surprise, a beautiful gift, a reminder that I serve a God who will always give me more me than I could ever ask or demand.

~

The hope you should give up
is the hope of being in charge.
Let God be God.
And he will bring you hope.

Words of Hope—
and Hope from
the Word

And God is able to make all grace abound to you, so that in all things at all times, having all that you need, you will abound in every good work.

—2 Corinthians 9:8

Now to him who is able to do immeasurably more than all we ask or imagine, according to his power that is at work within us, to him be glory in the church and in Christ Jesus throughout all generations, for ever and ever!

—Ephesians 3:20-21

What no eye has seen, nor ear heard, nor the human heart conceived, what God has prepared for those who love him.

—1 Corinthians 2:9 NRSV

When you give up all hope, you're probably only giving up the hope of getting your own outcome to happen. You're probably only giving up the hope that it will turn out that you actually have lots of power and input; that you are secretly God's West Coast representative. But it was when I was hopeless, caught in desperation and grief, that I got humble, teachable, willing to surrender. Of course, I grew up with an older brother, so to me surrender means you get your face ground in the dirt. It means you get noogies on your upper arm and then you have to go downstairs and get him oranges. But surrender to God means you come over to the winning side. A synonym for "surrender" is "yield," which means, agriculturally, to step aside and let something grow.

—Anne Lamott

Sometimes what you get turns out to be better than what you wanted in the first place.

—Eve Bunting

A few years ago someone asked me if my faith has changed since I've lost my three boys. I thought on that question for a while. Actually I think my faith has been altered since my boys died. My faith is no longer "sugar-coated." I have a greater respect for God and his sovereignty than I ever had before. I have a deeper faith now, but I also realize that God very likely has different plans for my life than I have. I know that God answers some of my prayers with a "no." He answers some with "yes," some with "wait a while," and some simply with "Trust me." I think the "Trust me" ones are the hardest....How thankful I am that God does know where he's taking each one of us, even when all we can do is trust.

—Marilyn Heavilin

Despair is always presumptous. How do we know what lies in the Great Not Yet or how some present "evil" may work itself out as a blessing in disguise? ...[I need to] be patient before I label any experience or close the door of hope. Despair is presumption, pure and simple, a going beyond what the facts at hand should warrant....The worst thing is never the last thing. God is already working on Plan B even as Plan A lies in shambles around our feet.

—John Claypool

10

Lampposts of Hope

*T*hey come as a gift of grace—those days when everything just seems to arrive together.

When your problems are still there, but not pressing—not getting in the way of your ability to enjoy life.

When you're blessed with enough energy and peace and creativity to feel you're getting somewhere.

When good things happen that cause you to smile and be joyful—the sunrise is beautiful, the clouds are fluffy and white, someone you love is with you, you accomplish something you really care about...or at least some of the above. When nothing really awful occurs, and the bad seems to slip into proper perspective.

Or sometimes, on the most special of days, when you experience one of those moments of pure clarity. When everything seems to slip into place and you know without a doubt that God is there beside you. You can almost see God breathe in the air around you.

Maybe you haven't had a day like that in a long time.

Or maybe you're in the middle of one right now.

Either way, if you want to live a hopeful life, I urge you to stop right now and give thanks for good days present and past—both the ordinary good days and the special, breathtaking, moment-of-truth good days. For I believe God gives us these days of grace to serve as lampposts of hope throughout our lives.

They're something to look forward to—for if God gives one good day, he's sure to give another (though what we consider a good day may change at different times in our lives).

And they're something to look back to—to fill our memories with joy, to remind us what we care about, to warm us with their reassurance that life can be good and God is indeed wonderful.

For me, at this time of my life, a good day is a little different than what it used to be. I can remember times when a good day included walking several miles, puttering around the house, antiquing with Bob, enjoying an elegant tea with my granddaughter Christine. Or it might have included a thrilling but exhausting schedule of speaking to women, hearing their concerns, praying and worshiping together, marveling that God was using what I had to give for his glory.

Right now, as I continue with my ongoing cancer treatment, a good day may simply be one when the constant pain of shingles—a debilitating side effect of a weakened immune system—is dulled. Just having my family around me and being able to enjoy them is enough to make a day worthwhile. So can going to a movie instead of trekking to the oncologist's office! Having the strength to enjoy simple pleasures can turn any day into a red-letter day.

And do you know what I've learned in this time when my good days are so different from what they used to be?

I've learned such days really *are* good if I receive them with gratitude and enjoyment. They're still a gift of grace given by a God who knows exactly what I need and wants to give it to me.

Then, if you want to live hopefully, don't waste your energy fretting that not all days are good days.

Don't spoil the joy by grousing that good days are not perfect days.

Accept your good days as they're given—as gifts of hope, as glimpses of heaven while we're still on earth, as reminders that even the best days of our lives are simply little tastes of the timeless joy that God has in store for us as we draw ever closer to him.

Accept them as shining lampposts dotted along our paths to help us see the way to God.

Here are some hope-giving things to do on a good day:

- *Give thanks, over and over again.* Recognize the rarity and beauty of the gift. Appreciate it. Store the moments in your memory.

- *Share the day with someone you love*—either by doing something together or telling somebody about it.

- *Capture the good day for the future* by writing in your journal, sketching the beauty around you, talking about it to your children.

- *When the day is over, let it go with good grace.* Smile and sigh and trust God for tomorrow.

∾

Hope can come from having a good day.

A Hopeful Hint

Make your mornings more hopeful by developing a morning ritual. First, put on your face—I guarantee you'll feel more hopeful. Then enjoy a quiet cup of coffee or tea and a bit of your favorite music—or just the songs of birds in your backyard. Ask God for the strength and courage to spend that day in hope.

*Words of Hope—
and Hope from
the Word*

*This is the day the LORD has made; let us rejoice
and be glad in it.*

—Psalm 118:24

*Hold fast the time! Guard it, watch over it, every
hour, every minute! Unregarded it slips away, like
a lizard, smooth, slippery. Hold every moment
sacred. Give each clarity and meaning, each the
weight of thine awareness, each its true and due
fulfillment.*

—Thomas Mann

*The past is history, the future is a mystery and
the moment is a gift. That is why it is called, "the
present."*

—Author unknown

Even blindfolded I would recognize the special-ness of this moment, and I see it with such focus that I almost have to turn my eyes away.

—Gloria Gaither

You will do well to pay attention to it, as to a light shining in a dark place, until the day dawns and the morning star rises in your hearts.

—2 Peter 1:19

Prayer increases our ability to accept the present moment. You cannot live in the future, you cannot live in the past, you can only live in the now. The present moment is already exactly as it ought to be, even if we do not understand why it is as it is.

—Matthew Kelly

Hope, child, tomorrow and tomorrow still,
  And every tomorrow hope; trust while you live.
Hope, each time the dawn doth heaven fill,
  Be there to ask as God is there to give.

—Victor Hugo

11

The Gift of a Terrible Day

$\mathcal{N}$ot too many years ago, a children's book by Judith Viorst appeared on the market and became an instant classic. It was called *Alexander and the Terrible, Horrible, No Good, Very Bad Day.* To my knowledge, it has never been out of print—and there's a reason for that. It's because every one of us knows what it's like to have that kind of awful day.

Maybe you're in one now—or you remember one all too vividly. A day when you feel physically terrible...or worse. When money is running low and the bills are piling up. When you have a fight with someone you care about—or you feel like picking one! When chores loom or bad news bites and you're not sure what fire to put out first...and you're not sure you're even interested in fighting fires.

"In this world you will have trouble," Jesus told us. That means we all have our quota of "terrible, horrible, no good, very bad" days. And that's not even to mention the "stop everything" kind of bad day when we sit at a deathbed or get the legal papers or hear the diagnosis.

Bad days are just a given in this fallen world. We might as well expect them. But can we find hope in them?

I honestly think so.

After all, one of two things is true about every bad day of our lives: Either we will live through it and be given a chance at another day…and that's reason for hope. Or we won't live through it, and we will have the opportunity to spend eternity with a heavenly Father who loves us. That, too, is reason for hope.

At different times of your life, bad days will be different. At some points of your life you look back at your previous bad days and think, *Why did I ever let all that bother me?* Or you might look back and think, *What a horrible time in my life! How did I ever live through that?* (But you did.)

Either way, what you'll see is that all those bad days were temporary. They all came in day-sized portions, and they all ended with a second chance, an opportunity for better days to follow. (Even the longest string of bad days eventually comes to an end.) Many of them, in addition, came with a hidden blessing—a word of encouragement that blossomed later into a relationship, a life lesson that finally clicked into place, a final confirmation that something really needed to change.

The point is, we serve a God of new beginnings. The hope he has for us is fresh every morning. So we can end our terrible, horrible, no good, very bad days with the expectation that God always has something better for us.

So thank God for the hope-giving grace of this awful day. Ask for the strength and courage to endure it, the wisdom to get through it without making other people suffer, the courage to learn and grow. And here are some things I've found helpful in surviving and learning from my own terrible, horrible, no good, very bad days:

- *Remind yourself that no matter what happens, twenty-four hours from now this day will be over!*

- *Marinate your heart in Scripture and prayer*—especially if you feel like you don't want to or don't have the time. Ask God to cut through your confusion and guide you step by step through the day.

- *Gripe a little bit to someone who cares*—because the support and prayers of someone who knows what you're going through can make all the difference.

- *Count to ten before you respond to anyone.* On bad days, your reactions tend to be off, and you could easily say something hurtful.

- *Pay a little extra attention to caring for yourself* on days when everything seems to go wrong. Try to get some exercise, to eat nutritious foods, to take your vitamins. And ask for help if you need it.

- *Ask yourself,* "Does God have something for me to learn on this terrible, horrible, no good, very bad day?"

Hope grows in a variety of circumstances—
including rotten days!

Words of Hope—
and Hope from
the Word

When I went to bed, Nick took back the pillow
he said I could keep. And the Mickey Mouse
nightlight burned out and I bit my tongue. The
cat wants to sleep with Anthony, not with me. It
has been a terrible, horrible, no good, very bad
day. My mom says some days are like that. Even
in Australia.

—Judith Viorst

Every day has its own particular brand of holiness to discover and worship appropriately.

—Annie Dillard

I cry aloud to the LORD;
* I lift up my voice to the LORD for mercy.*
I pour out my complaint before him;
* before him I tell my trouble.*
When my spirit grows faint within me,
* it is you who know my way.*

Psalm 142:1-3

But since we belong to the day, let us be self-controlled, putting on faith and love as a breastplate, and the hope of salvation as a helmet.

—1 Thessalonians 5:8

Let nothing disturb thee,
Let nothing affright thee.
All things are passing.
God never changes.

—St. Theresa of Avila

12

Stepping Out in Hope

*R*emember that movie *Romancing the Stone?* It starred Kathleen Turner as a big-city romance novelist who somehow became involved in a jungle adventure with Michael Douglas.

At the beginning of the movie, her imagination and her stories were full of romance and adventure, but her life was lonely, dull, and more or less empty.

At the end of the movie, though, she had actually moved out into the world and experienced the kind of romantic adventures she wrote about. She had tromped through tropical rainforests, slithered in mud down to a brown, snake-infested river, and fallen in love with an adventurous rogue. And though she had met with a lot of disappointments, something had changed in her.

"You're a hopeless romantic," said her editor, reading the draft of her latest novel.

"No," said the Kathleen Turner character, turning thoughtful. "I'm a *hopeful* romantic." (That was just before Michael Douglas showed up with a yacht—on a trailer, right in the middle of New York City!—ready to take her sailing into the sunset.)

Well, that movie was a fairy tale. But I think it also had something important to say about the way hope happens.

You see, what turned the Kathleen Turner character from a *hopeless* romantic to a *hopeful* one was the fact that she got out of her little room and, for the first time in her life, stopped living in her head. She stopped thinking wishfully and started living hopefully. She dared to get involved, to get her hands (and the rest of her) dirty. She took the risk of really living, and that made her more hopeful than ever before.

Now, I'm not saying you have to tromp through tropical rainforests and slither in the mud in order to find hope—yuck! But I do believe that a person becomes more hopeful not by simply wishing or wanting, but by actually *doing* something—by stepping out and getting involved in life.

Instead of wishing you could be thinner, you put on your tennies and take a walk. Instead of wishing for a friend, you ask an acquaintance to lunch. Instead of wishing you could make a difference, you sign up to help with Meals on Wheels or Habitat for Humanity or your church's prayer chain.

And yes, when you do that, you run the risk of being disappointed. You could pull a muscle. Or be rejected. Or discover that Meals on Wheels or Habitat or the prayer chain is not for you. Life does have the power to dash our hopes. But opting out of life is a far more potent hope destroyer than living life ever could be. For the more we hole up inside our safe little walls, avoiding conflict, minimizing our risk, the more we tend to lose our sense of the wonderful possibilities life has to offer. We never really know the strength hope has to offer until we step out and try something new.

Now, I know that stepping out may be hard to do when you're feeling shy or insecure or fearful and discouraged. You have to keep reminding yourself that hopeful feelings often follow hopeful acts.

But I have to be honest with you here. I'm not a natural adventurer. For most of my life, I would have been happy to putter around in my own little world and feather my own little nest. As a child, I was so shy that I once hid in a closet at my own birthday party! But again and again, God has confronted me with opportunities to step outside of myself and touch others. And when I've managed to say yes to God—saying yes to God is always a hopeful thing!—I've had so many amazing experiences.

If you had asked me forty years ago whether I would ever write a book or speak in front of a large audience of women or travel all over the country, I would have thought you were crazy. But it's happened! So much has happened I would never have believed. And as it's happened, my sense of hope has grown. When your life has changed as much as mine has over the last forty years, you start to believe that anything is possible.

So these days, I'm far from a hopeless romantic.

I'm not a hopeless anything.

Even now, when illness has narrowed my world a bit, I'm still a hopeful, wide-eyed child of God, just waiting to see what he has in mind for me next.

Take a chance, take a step—
and hope will follow.

Words of Hope—
and Hope from
the Word

How can God direct our steps if we're not taking
any?

—Sarah Leah Grafstein

Blessed are those whose strength is in you,
  who have set their hearts on pilgrimage.
As they pass through the Valley of Baca,
  they make it a place of springs;
  the autumn rains also cover it with pools.
They go from strength to strength,
  till each appears before God in Zion.
For the LORD God is a sun and shield;
  the LORD bestows favor and honor;
no good thing does he withhold
  from those whose walk is blameless.
O LORD Almighty,
  blessed is the [one] who trusts in you.

—Psalm 84:5-7,11,12

*If for some reason your eyes and ears become
blocked by pain or loss or depression then you
need to do something. Do whatever it takes, even
if it's difficult or expensive or inconvenient....Ask
for help if you need it. Beg for help if necessary.
But life is too short, relationships too precious,
God's messages too vital to risk not hearing them.*

—Don Osgood

*Become an answer to someone else's prayer.
Visit a sick relative or friend, call someone and
encourage them, mow a neighbor's yard, give your
spouse a back rub, write a check for a local
charity, compliment a coworker, volunteer at a
shelter for the homeless. Lift your spirits by lifting
someone else's load.*

—Tracy Mullins and Ann Spangler

Hope...is not a feeling; it is something you do.

—Katherine Paterson

13

The Process of a Miracle

*D*o you believe in miracles?

I do, more now than ever before. I believe that God is in the miracle business—that his favorite way of working is to pick up where our human abilities and understandings leave off and then do something so wondrous and unexpected that there's no doubt who the God is around here.

There are times in all our lives when we don't have any more tricks in our bags, when we turn a corner and find ourselves staring at dead ends. And that's when God's miracles start. I've seen it happen enough that counting on miracles is a big part of my hope.

But my understanding of how miracles happen has changed a little bit over the years—and especially in recent days.

Oh, I still believe we can trust God to accomplish what we humans assume is impossible. But now I'm more aware that he often does it in ways we don't expect. We may be looking for a magic show when God is arranging for a gradual healing. We may be expecting rescue from a cross when what God really has in mind is resurrection!

And if we're looking for only one kind of miracle, we might miss the wonder and hope of what God is doing in our lives.

So here are a few things to remember that might help keep your hope alive while you're waiting for a miracle.

First, you can trust God to take care of you and to answer your prayers. That's the bottom line, although most of us have to keep reminding ourselves of it. He will do what needs to be done, both through the natural processes of life (a miracle in itself) and through whatever supernatural intervention is necessary.

Second, keep reminding yourself that God does miracles on his terms, not ours—and for his own purposes. The people in Jesus' day were always clamoring for a miracle, and Satan tempted Christ in the wilderness with the opportunity to do miracles to order. But Jesus refused to do conjuring tricks on command. He did many miracles. But he was always responding to love, not to demand.

Today, too, God's miracles are for his purposes. Because he loves us, they are for our good as well. But they might not always take the form we would have chosen. We can pray for miracles—we *should* pray for miracles. But we can't custom-order the particular miracle we want. Instead, we must come to God with our need and expect him to meet it in the best way possible.

A third thing to remember is that God's miracles don't always work the way we expect. When you hear the word *miracle*, don't you usually think of something dramatic and instantaneous—or at least something clear-cut and measurable? The parting of the Red Sea or the raising of Lazarus—something with swooshing winds or leaping flames or blind people suddenly seeing or lame people leaping for joy?

Well, God is God, of course, and God sometimes does that. There are times when God intervenes directly and dramatically in ways that would play well on the big screen.

But it doesn't always happen that way. It doesn't *usually* happen that way.

More often, I believe, miracles unfold as part of a process. The very process of God's kingdom coming on earth is an ongoing miracle. God's work in the world is the process of miracle. He's transforming fallen people and hopeless circumstances into his kingdom on earth! He's in the continual process of restoration and redemption and healing and renewal. That's part of the process of miracle, too. If we want to be truly hopeful people, we need to keep watching to see how the miracles unfold.

But please understand. I'm not just saying that God only works his miracles through natural processes and other people. I believe he does intervene supernaturally in response to our prayers. He just doesn't always do it instantaneously.

Not long after I received my "forty-to-sixty percent, with a miracle" diagnosis, we decided to obey the directions in James 5 and be anointed with oil. Between the two services, we gathered in the office of the church we were attending. The elders of the church read Scriptures, anointed my forehead with olive oil, and prayed for my healing.

It was such a beautiful time. I felt wrapped in God's presence, even though I was in a lot of pain that day. I was crying from the beauty and tenderness of it all. My friend Yoli was crying. We were grabbing tissue after tissue for our running noses. And then, after it was over, Yoli looked at me, and I knew what she was thinking: "Are you healed yet?"

Well, I wasn't, not at that moment. In fact, I got a lot worse not long afterward.

But now, as I look back, that moment of anointing stands out in my mind as a turning point, the beginning of a process of healing not only my body, but also my mind and spirit.

Again and again, since that day, I have seen the miracles unfold—miracles of love in my relationship with Bob and the sacrificial service of my family and friends, miracles of patience and trust as I have learned to rest and wait instead of always yearning to get things done, miracles of transformation as I have felt my faith grow firmer and more confident. And yes, miracles of physical healing as I have moved toward remission in the process of my disease.

My doctor is much more optimistic today than he was on the day of that terrifying diagnosis. And I am more hopeful now than ever before that what God is going to do in whatever years I have remaining in my life is going to be wonderful.

I truly believe I have had my miracle. Every day I am living is a miracle.

And you are, too. I believe it with all my heart. Even now, a miracle of hope is unfolding in your heart. Trust it! Watch for it. You'll begin to see wondrous things unfolding in your life.

When we reach the end of our abilities,
God's possibilities are just beginning.

Words of Hope— and Hope from the Word

For him who has faith, the last miracle shall be greater than the first.

—Dag Hammarskjöld

Is any one of you in trouble? He should pray. Is anyone happy? Let him sing songs of praise. Is any one of you sick? He should call the elders of the church to pray over him and anoint him with oil in the name of the Lord. And the prayer offered in faith will make the sick person well; the Lord will raise him up. If he has sinned, he will be forgiven.

—James 5:13-15

*On the road to healing we see the tracks
of God in more and more things that occur—
in the people around us who begin to see God
in everything and who hear the silent language
of God in the simple words that are spoken....
We see God in the things we once thought
were commonplace. And in that attitude of life
we know we are never alone.*

—Don Osgood

*I will gladly accept the daily, life-sustaining
miracles. [They] are a promise from God to all
of us. If we live in his presence each day, we will
witness these miracles. We should never stop
praying for the "big miracle," but accepting the
small ones keeps us close to God and lets us
live joyfully.*

—Kathy Vertermark

*He performs wonders that cannot be fathomed,
miracles that cannot be counted.*

—Job 5:9

14

Hands on My Heart

It's just a handprint traced on a piece of paper, with a simple heart shape drawn upon the hand.

It almost looks like a kindergartener's drawing.

But to me, it's become a potent picture of hope—because it's a reminder of what can happen when God's children unite in love and prayer.

I started using the "heart on hand" quite a few years ago, when I began using a notebook to organize my prayer times. I decided to make a separate page for each of my precious grandchildren, and I asked each grandchild to trace a handprint on his or her personal page. We drew a heart on each handprint, and I let the children decorate their pages. After that, when I prayed for each of them, I would put my own hand on top of their little handprint. That simple device helped me tune in on them, to focus my prayers. I could feel the connection between us strengthen as "hand on hand" I took those babies to the Lord in prayer.

My "heart on hand" prayer pages were so meaningful to me that soon I had asked to make handprints of others who were

dear to me. My husband, Bob, of course. My children. My
dear friends. Each had a special page in my notebook—and a
special place of prayer in my heart.

When a close friend of our daughter's was about to enter
the hospital for a bone-marrow transplant, I hosted a small
luncheon for her. After lunch, we had her trace her hand on
five sheets of paper—one for each guest. We all drew heart
shapes on the handprints and decorated the pages. Then we
each placed our hands on hers and prayed for her healing. We
took the handprints home and posted them on the refrigera-
tor door as a reminder to place our hands on "hers" and pray.

What a deeply meaningful expression of love and support
that was! As we prayed for Lynn's healing, we were drawn
closer together as well. All of us, sick and well, felt the power
of that prayerful connection.

Over the years, after that, the little picture of a heart on a
hand has stayed with me. I still use it in my prayer notebook. I
have taught it to children and shared the idea with women in
seminars. It was a great image! But I had no idea how meaningful it would become to me when I in turn became ill. For
that same little heart-on-hand symbol would be a powerful
tool God used to give me hope through the prayers of others:

When I was diagnosed with cancer and began that long,
confusing journey through treatment, Bob and I were deeply
touched by the support we felt. So many people called and

wrote and offered to pray for me that it was a challenge just to keep up communication.

So what I did was trace my hand on a sheet of paper.

Then I drew a little heart on that hand, and I added a hopeful Scripture verse and a little summary of what was going on with my cancer.

We made copies of that simple little sheet of paper and sent it out to all the people who had offered to pray—we even posted copies on our website (www.emiliebarnes.com). We asked friends and family to place their hands on mine and pray for my healing. And they have! They have told me so. I have also felt their prayers as a cushion of hope that has carried me through many difficult days. How it has lifted my heart to picture all those people out there praying with their hand on mine.

Now, I know it's only a visual aid—a symbol, a reminder.

I know that the power of prayer doesn't depend on handprints drawn on paper.

But what that little handprint does for both the pray-er and the pray-ee is to remind us that we are bonded together in love and prayer. That not only are our hearts beating as one in that moment of communion, but we are all held together in the mighty hands of the Father, who cares for us all.

～

Hope comes from living in
the communion of prayer.

Words of Hope— and Hope from the Word

If a care is too small to be turned into a prayer, it is too small to be made into a burden.

—Corrie ten Boom

Teach us how to pray with the compassion which is not afraid to suffer with those who suffer and, if need be, to enter into the darkness with them.

—Elizabeth Goudge

Whatever you ask for in prayer with faith, you will receive.

—Matthew 21:22

More things are wrought by prayer than this world dreams of, wherefore, let thy voice rise like a fountain for me night and day.

—Alfred, Lord Tennyson

*Prayer is...a mine which is never exhausted....
It is the root, the fountain, the mother of a
thousand blessings.*

—John Chrysostom

*I always thank my God as I remember you in my
prayers, because I hear about your faith in the
Lord Jesus and your love for all the saints. I pray
that you may be active in sharing your faith, so
that you will have a full understanding of every
good thing we have in Christ. Your love has given
me great joy and encouragement, because you,
brother, have refreshed the hearts of the saints.*

—Philemon 1:4-7

Prayer is a long rope with a strong hold.

—Harriet Beecher Stowe

*As white snowflakes fall quietly and thickly on a
winter day, answers to prayer will settle down
upon you at every step you take.... The story of
your life will be the story of prayer and answers
to prayer.*

—Ole Hallesby

15

Strong Hope

I learned something interesting when I started looking for Scripture verses about hope. I guess I expected a lot of verses about hope and joy, hope and happiness, hope and love—you know, all those nice, warm, uplifting qualities that makes us feel good just to think of them.

But I didn't expect to see so many verses about hope and strength. Hope and endurance. Hope and courage. Again and again in the Bible, hope is linked with muscular, almost macho, words that hint of hard times and suffering.

"Be of good courage," writes the psalmist. "And he shall strengthen your heart, all you who hope in the LORD" (Psalm 31:24 NKJV).

"What strength do I have, that I should hope?" complains Job. (See Job 6:11 NKJV.)

"But we also rejoice in our sufferings," the apostle Paul reminds us in the book of Romans, "because we know that suffering produces perseverance; perseverance, character; and character, hope" (Romans 5:3,4).

Strength. Courage. Endurance. They're not really what used to come to mind when I thought of hope. But they fit. In fact, the longer I live, the more I understand how appropriate they are.

The truth is, it takes strength to keep on hoping through good days and bad ones. Sometimes believing in tomorrow takes all the mental and emotional and even physical power we can muster and more. It's a matter of doing what we think God wants us to do, trusting that we will be given the strength we need when we need it.

It's an act of courage to keep on hoping when circumstances seem dark and progress seems impossible. It takes courage to go against the cynicism that surrounds us and believe the best about the future. It takes courage to confront Satan's lies and our own negative emotions—our discouragement, our disappointments—and keep trusting in God's hopeful promises. It's an act of courage to keep on hoping when circumstances seem dark and progress seems impossible.

And never underestimate the endurance required to keep on hoping over the long haul. Fatigue and despair so often walk hand in hand. When you get really tired, the tendency is to give up on hoping. To focus only on your aching feet and burning muscles, losing sight of where you're walking and why.

But here's the other side of the connection between hope and strength that makes it all work.

Yes, hope requires strength—sometimes all the strength you can muster. But hope also *gives* you strength. Hope energizes. Hope moves you forward. When you dare to hope, you can do so much more than you ever thought.

And yes, hope requires courage—but hoping can make you brave. It makes the sacrifices seem worthwhile.

And hope certainly requires endurance. But hope helps you endure. Hope will carry you farther through suffering and trials than almost any quality. For hope is often the thing that kicks in to endure when physical, emotional, and mental strength is gone. It's one of those seemingly fragile qualities that endure when more robust attitudes have failed.

The poet Emily Dickinson once suggested that hope is a "thing with feathers" that keeps on singing no matter what happens. I think of it as more like a monarch butterfly or a hummingbird—those seemingly delicate little creatures that migrate millions of miles a year, flying through rain, wind, and snow to reach their destination. It may seem fragile, but it's enduring. And it's brave. And therefore it's remarkably strong.

And here's the truth that makes it all work: We're not expected to come up with the strength and courage and endurance on our own. In fact, we're not expected to be strong at all. We get our strong hope, our courageous hope, our enduring hope, by depending in the Lord, who is our strength.

But it doesn't just come to us by sitting there, waiting to be strong so we can move forward in hope. The way it usually works is that we just start doing what we think God wants us to do, trusting that we will be given the strength we need when we need it. Like the hummingbird or the monarch, we just start doing what we need to do.

That's when the power of the Lord kicks in, and hope starts to sing.

❧

Hope is always stronger than you think.
Trust it—and you will find the strength
and courage you need.

Words of Hope— and Hope from the Word

But I will sing of your strength,
  in the morning I will sing of your love;
for you are my fortress,
  my refuge in times of trouble.
O my Strength, I sing praise to you;
  you, O God, are my fortress, my loving God.

—Psalm 59:16-17

Thus grave these lessons on thy soul—
  Hope, faith, and love; and thou shalt find
Strength when life's surges rudest roll,
  Light when thou else wert blind!

—Johann Christoph Friedrich von Schiller

It is pain and weakness and constant failures
which keep me from pride and help me to grow.
The power of God is to be found in weakness,
but it is God's power.

—Madeleine L'Engle

We must never forget that today's legendary achievements—awesome as they may seem—were yesterday's risky adventures. Courage is not the capacity never to be afraid; as Karl Barth reminds us, "Courage is fear that has said its prayers." Hear, then, the promise: There is help to be had from God. You can count on it. It might take the form of ecstasy, when you "mount up with wings as eagles." It could come in the form of energy, when you "run and are not weary." Or then again, it may be simply the strength to "walk and not faint." This latter may seem like a little thing, but when you are really "up against it," when you have no occasion to soar and no room to run, believe me, it is not. In those moments, the gifts of endurance and patience become utterly important—just to stay on your feet and not give up. And I can say out of honest experience that if you are willing "to wait upon the Lord" and accept this gift, you will not be disappointed.

—John Claypool

In the battles most of us are facing, there are only two options where being courageous is concerned—and turning around and going back is not one of them. We can choose to live through the days before us, or we can choose not to live. Choosing not to live is cowardly....No matter what it is that brings you to a difficult place— death, illness, divorce, or even betrayal—God intends for you to leave it with new life. And it is not your own strength that will bring it forth.

—Sandy Clough

But he said to me, "My grace is sufficient for you, for my power is made perfect in weakness." Therefore I will boast all the more gladly about my weaknesses, so that Christ's power may rest on me. That is why, for Christ's sake, I delight in weaknesses, in insults, in hardships, in persecutions, in difficulties. For when I am weak, then I am strong.

—2 Corinthians 12:9-10

16

Telling Stories

$\mathcal{R}$emember when..."

Children just love to play that game. They love to hear and tell and retell family stories, memorizing the particular set of happenings and experiences that made the family what it is.

"Tell me about when I..." The stories of their own past tell them how they got where they are.

"I remember when we..." The stories of their own experiences help them understand how they fit in now.

"Why do we..." The explanations of family traditions help them get a feel for who they are and where they're going.

It's no accident that most children are hopeful creatures.

Children understand instinctively that hope for tomorrow is built on memories of yesterday.

In other words, though hope is a forward-looking quality, it is strengthened by looking backward—especially when we look backward with eyes of faith. The more you look back in gratitude for what God has done for you in the past, and the more you retell the stories of his work in your life, the more easily you'll believe that God will do good things in the future.

Our memories can be so short, sometimes—and I'm not talking about forgetting where we put the car keys! We forget so easily the laws God has given us for our own benefit, the guidelines that are intended to help us live in hope. We forget as well the gifts of grace that shape our lives—the miracles of help and encouragement and redemption that keep us moving around and between and beyond the barriers in our lives. And this forgetfulness is one of the primary reasons we lose hope.

And so it's important to look back and remember. It's important to tell and retell the stories of who we were and what God has done in our lives and what he requires of us. The more care we take in preserving these tales of how God has worked in the past, the more powerful and realistic our hope will be—and the more hope we'll be able to share with others.

"Remember when I lost my job, and the kids were in college, and you weren't sure what you wanted to do next—and that radio interview led to a whole new career for both of us?" (That actually happened to us, years ago!)

"Remember how our dream house became available just when we were on the market?" (That happened to us, too.)

"Remember how we finally closed on this beach house— then discovered that the oncologist everyone was recommending practices only in this area?" (That's a more recent miracle. The doctor said he would not be able to treat me from our inland home in Riverside. And it just so happened we were already in the process of setting up housekeeping just miles from his office!)

It really works. As we tell each other such stories, recounting the times we've seen God work in our lives—our discouragement fades and our hope grows more confident.

My Bob has done this for me so often during the past few years. When I was discouraged by the fear of yet another treatment or the frustration of dealing with insurance companies or the irritation of just not being able to do the things I used to do, Bob would remind me, "God has brought us this far. He won't abandon us now." And as I remembered, I found the courage and hope to go on. If God could do so much for us in the past, surely he has nothing but good in mind for the future.

But it's not only our personal memories that can bring us hope. When I hear how God has worked in somebody else's life, I begin to gain hope that he can do the same thing for me. That's really all a personal witness or testimony is—a sharing of personal memories of God's work in an individual's life.

And the Bible does this for me as well. Have you ever thought of God's Word as a memory book? That's one of the primary functions of the Bible—to bring hope by telling and retelling the stories of how God has worked in the lives of his people. Large portions of the Old Testament consist of the story of God's work among the Hebrew people. The Gospels and the book of Acts and even parts of the epistles are basically stories of how Jesus changed everything. And all these stories are, in essence, reminders that we always have hope.

So do you want more hope in your life? One of the most helpful things you can do is to begin working on a "hope history." You can do this on paper, on a computer, on tape, or even with another person. The point is to begin paying attention to your own stories.

Don't put a lot of pressure on yourself. Just begin looking at your earliest memory, then let that memory lead to another. You'll be amazed at what comes up. In fact, the more you tell your story to yourself and others, the more memories will start popping into your head. Some may bring pain. Some you might prefer not to visit, and that's all right. But as you think about your past, try to look for patterns of grace that emerge from your memories:

- Amazing turns or unexpected graces that have increased your faith.

- People who have shaped your life and taught you to hope—your mother, your father, your children, your friends.

- Lessons you've learned that you can pass on to others.

- True stories from others that have boosted your own hope.

- Things you've read that have changed your thinking or opened your eyes.

- Moments of insight or understanding that have changed the direction of your life.

- Events or experiences that have new meaning in hindsight.

As you sort through your memories, pray for the discernment to understand how God has brought you to where you are today. And it can also be helpful to rely on the gift of other people's insight. I can't tell you how many times I've been helped by a friend who was able to show me what God was doing in my life. When my vision became muddied and confused, my friend was able to show me a clearer picture, and that gave me hope.

Above all, try to look back on your life with thanksgiving. A sense of gratitude for God's presence in our lives will help open our eyes to what he has done in the past and what he will do in the future.

While you're looking back, though, don't forget to pay attention to the present. If your heart is tuned to see God's working today, you'll be more apt to remember tomorrow—to be hopeful!

~

Your whole life can be a story of hope
if you learn how to hear it and tell it.

Words of Hope— and Hope from the Word

Humans…have history, memory, and hope. Remembering is the root of trust, hoping is the center of faith.

—Martin Marty

I will remember the deeds of the LORD;
  yes, I will remember your miracles of long ago.
I will meditate on all your works
  and consider all your mighty deeds.
Your ways, O God, are holy.
What god is so great as our God?
You are the God who performs miracles;
  you display your power among the peoples.
With your mighty arm you redeemed your people.

—Psalm 77:11-15

I will utter hidden things, things from of old—
  what we have heard and known,
  what our fathers have told us.
We will not hide them from their children;
  we will tell the next generation
the praiseworthy deeds of the LORD,
  his power, and the wonders he has done.
He decreed statutes for Jacob
  and established the law in Israel,
which he commanded our forefathers
  to teach their children,
so the next generation would know them,
  even the children yet to be born,
  and they in turn would tell their children.
Then they would put their trust in God
  and would not forget his deeds
  but would keep his commands.

—Psalm 78:2-7

107

God's goodness hath been good to thee:
Let never day nor night unhallow'd pass,
But still remember what the Lord hath done.

—William Shakespeare

Memories are powerful things, capable of holding
a family together or tearing it apart. In the end,
after all, memories are all we really have of each
other. We should, therefore, treat them as precious gifts that we are allowed to give the ones
we love.

—Angela L. Sharp

17

Stripped for Action

$\mathcal{H}$ave you ever felt that life is stripping you bare—shaking you up and changing you all around so that you hardly recognize your life?

New mothers can feel that way—as the new baby turns everything topsy-turvy. So can people in midlife who are facing empty nests, midlife crises, or menopause. Old age can bring with it a series of losses—physical strength, active vocation, a procession of funerals. And major life events at any age—a move, a new job, a bereavement, a health crisis—can bring on a series of changes that leave us feeling vulnerable and disoriented...and easily discouraged.

All this can be an upsetting. It *is* upsetting. But those times when life strips you bare can also be liberating, hope-filled times if you keep yourself open to what God is trying to do in your life.

There was a time in my early forties when I suddenly woke up in an empty nest. For nearly twenty years, I had poured all my energies into making a comfortable, nurturing home for my children—and now, suddenly, I was out of a job. I was at a loss for what to do with myself. And to make things worse, my Bob was in the process of closing out his business. We had no idea what would happen to us next.

What happened was a totally unforeseen career for both of us—as writers, speakers, and the owners of our own small business.

Then there was a time in my late fifties when illness finally brought me to my knees. After years of soldiering on, I realized I had to stop. I had to back out of commitments and dedicate myself to the work of healing. We even moved to be closer to my doctor. So there I was—suddenly without my career, without my health and energy—I didn't even have my familiar, well-loved kitchen! And Bob, whose work was integrally involved with mine, was out of a job, too!

What happened then was…well, I don't know exactly, because we're still in the middle of that one. But what we can see so far is a deepening of our love and trust for each other, an intensification of our desire to be a blessing to others, and—interestingly enough—a freshening of our hope.

Somehow, in the midst of being stripped of everything familiar, we were experiencing fresh infusions of hope. We don't know what's going to happen next, but we just have a sense that God has something amazing in mind for us—something we can't even imagine yet. To prepare us, he's setting us free from a lot of our previous involvements.

Other people who have gone through such stripped-down times have told me they've felt the same thing. The more their life changed, in fact, the stronger their hope grew.

Maybe it was because when we are stripped of our everyday allegiances and involvements, we know that we come face to face once more with the Lord—and he is really our only Hope.

If you're at one of those "stripping" times of life, maybe you'll find this helpful to realize. Don't despair when it feels like everything's been taken away. Instead, tell yourself that the process of being stripped down may well be God's process of getting you ready for something new and wonderful.

Don't fight what's going on in your life.

Instead, let yourself listen and be still.

Seek the Lord more diligently in prayer.

Read his Word expectantly.

Envision yourself being stripped for action—sleek, beautiful, ready to do his will.

∾

Some things have to die in order for new life (and new hope) to happen. But remember that with God, death is never the last word.

Words of Hope—
and Hope from
the Word

I tell you the truth, unless a kernel of wheat falls to the ground and dies, it remains only a single seed. But if it dies, it produces many seeds.

—John 12:24

My hope, each day as I grow older, is that this will never be simply chronological aging—which is a nuisance and frequently a bore…but that I will also grow into maturity, where the experience which can be acquired only through chronology will teach me how to be more aware, open, unafraid to be vulnerable, involved, committed, to accept disagreement without feeling threatened (repeat and underline this one), to understand that I cannot take myself seriously until I stop taking myself seriously—to be, in fact, a true adult.

—Madeleine L'Engle

Consider it pure joy, my brothers, whenever you face trials of many kinds, because you know that the testing of your faith develops perseverance. Perseverance must finish its work so that you may be mature and complete, not lacking anything.

—James 1:2-4

"I'm being dismantled," I told a friend not long ago. "God has me stripped down to the chassis, and I'm shivering and cold." I felt as though my fleshly parts lay scattered all around me with only my frame left propped up on blocks. It was all I could do to fight the temptation to reassemble myself; to pick up my old ways and settle back into old, familiar patterns. But I didn't want to miss what God had in mind. It would be a tragedy to go through so much discomfort and come out unchanged, I decided. The only logical choice was to wait, to stay there, stripped and broken; until the master Mechanic finished his work.

—Joanna Weaver

For we know in part and we prophesy in part, but when perfection comes, the imperfect disappears. When I was a child, I talked like a child, I thought like a child, I reasoned like a child. When I became a man, I put childish ways behind me. Now we see but a poor reflection as in a mirror; then we shall see face to face. Now I know in part; then I shall know fully, even as I am fully known.

—1 Corinthians 13:9-12

A child asks, "Where did I come from?" A teenager asks, "What shall I do?" The mature person asks, "What shall I become?" It is a little like looking into a kaleidoscope—when we hold it up to our eye, the beautiful pattern almost takes our breath away. But unless we turn it, we'll miss the beautiful design that comes with the change. This is what life is meant to be like for the growing Christian. As we change and mature, life becomes increasingly beautiful with each change.

—Dale Evans Rogers

18

A Hope Transplant

*H*ere's something important I've discovered about hope in the past few years. Or rediscovered—because I knew it before, but it's much more real to me now.

Hope comes from God. That's the bottom-line truth. But the way he most often chooses to share that gift with us is through other people.

Hope grows stronger when it's shared. That's just the way it works. It can be caught, almost like a good disease. It has the strange ability to grow when it's divided. And it can be transferred deliberately from one person to another—just like blood can be transfused and kidneys, eyeballs, and bone marrow can be transplanted.

Now, you might think a "hope transplant" is an odd idea. But that's exactly what happened to Lisa Bergan of Wichita Falls, Texas. I heard about Lisa through my editor, who read her story in the newspaper.[1] It's stuck in my mind ever since, partly because Lisa and I have similar illnesses, but mostly because her story illustrates so beautifully the way hope can be given from one person to another.

---

1. Lynda Stringer, "Tree helps woman pay for bone marrow transplant," *Wichita Falls Times Record News*, December 13, 1999.

You see, Lisa's leukemia had progressed to the point that she was in need of a bone marrow transplant. And she had other needs as well. For one thing, she needed money; although her medical insurance would cover the transplant, there were a host of other things it wouldn't cover, including the cost of harvesting the bone marrow. Lisa also needed practical support while recovering from the transplant—cooking, cleaning, and just being there when she was weak. And Lisa needed a family to love her and support her. But Lisa was single and childless. Her parents were dead. And her only relative, a brother, lived half a continent away.

Not surprisingly, Lisa had reached the point where she was running out of hope. She told that to a friend at her church.

"Don't worry," said the friend. "I've got hope enough for both of us." And right then and there, the idea for Lisa's hope transplant was born. Before long, the whole church had rallied around her for the purpose of helping and giving her hope.

Because it was early December, they decided to use the Advent season as a time to focus on helping Lisa with her needs. An "Advent Hope Transplant Tree" was set up in the church lobby and covered with cut-out ornaments. Each ornament represented an opportunity for church members to pledge either money or practical support—transportation to the hospital, meals, nursing care, whatever was needed.

By the time the article was written, the Hope Transplant Tree had raised $3200, plus many other pledges of help. But it was emotional help that was making the biggest difference in Lisa's life. "I have no family other than my brother so I've been adopted by the church. They've become my parents, my grandparents, my aunts, uncles and sisters," she said. "It's so overwhelming the things they've done for me and the support they've given me." In the process, she said, her faith had grown as well as her hope. "When you're facing an illness or a circumstance God really comes through and provides," Lisa said. "When I've needed finances, there's been finances there; when I needed people, people have sprouted up around me. It's incredible."

I don't know the end of Lisa's story. I don't know if her bone marrow transplant was a success. But I am confident that her hope transplant was working—because I've been experiencing hope transplants almost every day since I became ill.

They have come in so many ways. Through phone calls and cards. Through the prayers of people who petition God for my healing. Through my Bob's determined optimism and physical care. Through the empathy and wisdom of people who have been through what I was going through. Through dear friends who were willing to just crawl up on the bed beside me and cry with me.

Again and again, through my family and friends and brothers and sisters in Christ, I've received both hope *transfusions*—fresh bursts of hope and optimism—and hope *transplants*—deeper, sacrificial donations of love and dedication that give me the strength to make some hope of my own.

The interesting thing about all this transfer of hope, though, is that it doesn't just flow in one direction. For the people who give of themselves to transfer hope to another person almost always receive a fresh supply of hope themselves.

That's what the members of Lisa Bergan's church discovered. That's what my hope-transferring friends have told me. And that's what I've discovered, for even during my time of illness I've had the privilege of donating some hope of my own to others. (It is my deep desire that this book will be a form of hope transplant for you.)

For it is the very process of sharing hope—of loving each other, encouraging each other, building up each other, helping each other in practical ways—that produces more and more hope in all of us.

It comes from God.

But it grows and grows as we transfuse it and transplant it and pass it from heart to heart.

~

Hope grows as we pass along love
and help to one another.

A Hopeful Hint

Have you ever tried to commit a random act of kindness—doing something nice and unexpected for a stranger, such as scraping her windshield or paying her toll? You'd be surprised at the feelings of hope such an act can generate. You'll end up feeling that the world isn't so bad after all.

Words of Hope— and Hope from the Word

A cup that is already full cannot have more added to it. In order to receive the further good to which we are entitled, we must give of that which we have.

—Margaret Becker

Above all, love each other deeply, because love covers over a multitude of sins. Offer hospitality to one another without grumbling. Each one should use whatever gift he has received to serve others, faithfully administering God's grace in its various forms.

—1 Peter 4:8-10

Then the righteous will answer him, "Lord, when did we see you hungry and feed you, or thirsty and give you something to drink? When did we see you a stranger and invite you in, or needing clothes and clothe you? When did we see you sick or in prison and go to visit you?" The King will reply, "I tell you the truth, whatever you did for one of the least of these brothers of mine, you did for me."

—Matthew 25:37-40

I never look at the masses as my responsibility. I look at the individual. I can love only one person at a time. I can feed only one person at a time. Just one, one, one. You get closer to Christ by coming closer to each other.

—Mother Teresa of Calcutta

19

You Can Always Do Something

*T*here's nothing more discouraging than not being able to do what you really want to do.

Children, who are small and dependent, understand that very well.

Elderly people, living with fixed incomes and physical decline, often come to realize this.

Sick people often find it easier to face physical pain than the emotional pain of not being able to do as much as they once could.

And we all face times when we slam our faces into our own inadequacy, when what we can do and what we wish we could do just don't come together.

And feeling inadequate can do a number on hope.

In situations like that, it's helped me a lot to realize that while there's a lot I can't do, if I have a heart of love, I can always do something.

Here's an example that happened to me recently.

A year or so ago, I was scheduled to speak at a women's conference in Georgia put on by Bailey Smith Ministries. Unfortunately, that was about the time my cancer was finally diagnosed and I had to begin my first round of chemotherapy, so I had to reluctantly cancel.

Do you know what those wonderful people did then? They called the people at DaySpring, who donated 1200 get-well cards. And then they asked every single woman at the conference to write me a card! They gathered all the cards together into a big gift-wrapped box and mailed it to me.

Well, all I could feel when I saw that box was dread! That may sound ungracious. But you see, it's always been important to me to respond to acts of kindness. And all I could think when I saw that box was, "Now I've got to write a thank-you note!" I just couldn't face it. I was too weak. So I left the box sitting there. I didn't even open it.

After a few weeks, it was still sitting there. I thought, "I've got to deal with this box." So I opened it, and out flew the 1200 hand-addressed greeting cards, all with my name on the front, spelled correctly, a miracle in itself!

Well, now I felt even worse. There was no way I could even read through all those cards. I opened about ten of them. Each had a lovely, handwritten note. Several were from women who themselves were in ill health or facing other problems.

Now I was really down. I could feel a cloud of discouragement just hanging over me. I wanted so much to respond to the huge act of kindness that those cards represented, but I knew I didn't have the strength to write back to any of these women. In my current weakness, there was nothing I could do.

Except…

In the quiet of the afternoon, as I sat clutching that little batch of cards, the idea came to me.

There *was* something I could do to give back to all those women who cared enough to write me.

I just took those ten cards in my hand and prayed for the women who had written them. Then I put them aside and went on with my day.

The next day, I took ten more cards, read them, and prayed for their senders. That was all. Just ten cards. But the next day I read and prayed over ten more. I kept that up until I had worked my way through all 1200 of them.

And the more I read, the more I prayed, the more hope filled my heart. Before I knew it, the heavy cloud of discouragement had melted away.

There is *always* something you can do, even if that something is very small. If you can give up your pride enough to do not what you wish you could, but what you can—that very act of doing will give you hope.

I promise.

~

There is always something you can do—
and doing it will bring you hope.

Words of Hope— and Hope from the Word

We don't have to look forward to big things. I have a friend who says we need to look forward to something. For her it can be thinking about buying a new pair of shoes. Many women like to go "shopping." Perhaps that's psychologically related to the human need to look forward to something exciting and meaningful.

—Bill Kinnaird

We can do no great things—only small things with great love.

—Mother Teresa

I am only one; but still I am one. I cannot do everything, but still I can do something; I will not refuse to do the something I can do.

—Helen Keller

"Leave her alone," said Jesus. "Why are you bothering her? She has done a beautiful thing to me. …She did what she could."

—Mark 14:6,8

"The mustard seed," said Jesus, "is the smallest of all seeds." Yet it grows into an enormous tree. And so it is with our lives. Each tiny part can be a seedbed where faith brings God's word alive. Our small things become his big things, our tiny offerings his kingdom's treasure, our widow's mites his riches in glory.

—Betty Pulkingham

Nothing that is worth doing can be achieved in our lifetime; therefore we must be saved by hope. Nothing that is true or beautiful makes complete sense in any immediate context of history; therefore we must be saved by faith. Nothing we do, however virtuous, can be accomplished alone; therefore we must be saved by love. No virtuous act is quite as virtuous from the standpoint of our friend or foe as it is from our standpoint. There, we must be saved by the final form of love which is forgiveness.

—Reinhold Niebuhr

20

A Shot of Hope

*H*ave you ever come down with a case of hopelessness and despair that hits you almost like the flu?

It can work that way. In fact, if we keep in mind that hope is the normal, healthy state of the human soul, it's easy to understand that hopelessness is a kind of spiritual disease. It can really get us down. It can even be fatal if we get a bad enough case.

But the good news is that our God is a God of healing. Whether the disease is measles, cancer, the common cold, or plain old despair, he provides us with both natural and supernatural defenses both to fight it and to build up our defenses against it.

This means that if you can come down with hopelessness, you can also inoculate yourself against it. Not with a needle and vaccine, but with a series of attitudes and habits that help keep despair from invading your spirit. If you prepare these "inoculations" in times of hope, you'll be a lot less likely to "come down with" despair when life gets hard.

How do you inoculate yourself with hopefulness? Here are some things I've discovered:

- *Be aware of God's goodness.* Try to notice what God is doing in your life. Notice when he keeps his promises, when you are aware of his presence, when you feel his love. If you can, write down what you notice. Your awareness of God's hopeful acts in the present will become future memories to keep you healthy.

- *Appreciate the good things in your life.* Open your arms to accept and appreciate and enjoy God's good gifts. Taste and see how good God is.

- *Invest in healthy relationships.* When your own hope fails, you can be revived by the hope you've given to others.

- *Keep short accounts.* Don't let guilt and resentment fester too long; they'll just drag you down. Be quick to confess sin and ask forgiveness.

- *Soak up God's Word.* Make it a part of you so it's in your heart when you need it.

- *Practice prayer.* By keeping in close touch with the God of hope, you'll be much less likely to succumb to despair.

There may still be times, of course, when despite all these preventive measures you find your spirits sinking. Sometimes physical illness might even drag you down into depression or discouragement. But when that happens, the "treasure" you stored up with your preventive measures—your good relationships, your vibrant prayer life, your intimacy with God's Word—will still be there with you, assisting in your quick return to health.

Nothing will be wasted. And hope and health will soon be yours once more.

~

You are invited to participate in your own hopeful health.

 ## *A Hopeful Hint*

Hopeful feelings often follow hopeful acts. You can build a storehouse of hope in your heart by starting something that will take some time to mature. Here are some ideas:

- *Begin a new craft project.*

- *Invite a new acquaintance to lunch or coffee.*

- *Make tomorrow's to-do list.*

- *Hang new curtains in your kitchen.*

- *Read to preschoolers in a daycare, or volunteer to help with the high school choir.*

- *Pick up trash at a nearby lake.*

- *Plan a reunion of one or two old friends.*

- *Take lessons in something you've never done—playing guitar, speaking Norwegian, kickboxing, or calligraphy.*

- *Offer to teach a class in something you do well—guitar, Spanish, journalism, scrapbooking.*

- *Schedule thirty minutes a day for a week to begin tackling an "impossible" task that's bringing you down—cleaning the storeroom, reorganizing your files, going through your old clothes.*

Words of Hope— and Hope from the Word

Whoever the agent may be, the healer is God, and he seems to like variety and to exercise considerable imagination. One day he used the stirred waters of a pool for healing, and on another he made a paste with earth and spittle and anointed the eyes of a blind man.

—Elizabeth O'Connor

Why are you downcast, O my soul?
  Why so disturbed within me?
Put your hope in God,
  for I will yet praise him,
  my Savior and my God.

—Psalm 42:11

Health is not simply the absence of sickness.

—Hannah Green

"But I will restore you to health and heal your wounds," declares the LORD.

—Jeremiah 30:17

131

My Dear Child,
Are you hurting today? Under all the coping mechanisms you've set up to keep your life in motion, is there a place in you that is bruised and aching, a hidden place in need of healing? I know. I can see. I want to heal you.

It is to the downtrodden and the broken that I came. Let me in. Don't hide the wounded places. Don't show me only the shiny achievements and the competent areas of your life. I am here for the hurt in you, too. I want to bring health to every part of you.

Compassionately yours, God

—Claire Cloninger

Deep peace of the running wave to you.
Deep peace of the flowing air to you.
Deep peace of the quiet earth to you.
Deep peace of the shining stars to you.
Deep peace of the gentle night to you.
Moon and stars pour their healing light on you.
Deep peace of Christ, the light of the world
   to you.
Deep peace to you.

—Ancient Irish rune, adapted by John Rutter

21

Fruit and Seeds

*W*e've always loved fruit at our house. I like to keep a big wooden bread bowl full of it on our counter—apples, pears, lemons, avocadoes. When we prepare lunch or breakfast, we always try to include slices of sweet, delicious, healthful fruit.

One of the things we're always aware of when we deal with fruit is seeds. Well, not in the oranges—since our Riverside, California, home is the location of the world's first navel orange tree. But you can't cut into most fruits without encountering seeds. Big, burly seeds in the avocadoes. Stringy, slimy clusters of seeds in pumpkins and cantaloupes. Little brown apple seeds. Tough white lemon seeds.

In fact, when you think of it, the seed is the real point of the fruit—because it's the seed that's the future and hope of the plant.

Fruit, in a sense, is the prerequisite of hope.

I think that's interesting to consider when we talk about finding hope in our lives.

Jesus told us specifically, in his parable of the vine, that when we stay closely attached to him our lives will produce fruit. He also said that we're basically worthless to him if there's no fruit. The fifth chapter of Galatians even spells out some of the fruit that grows in us when we live in Christ.

And you've heard of all this before, of course. But have you ever stopped to think that this spiritual fruit in our lives will carry seeds, too? It just makes sense. The more fruit there is, the more seeds there will be…and the more hope will fill our hearts.

Do you want hope to grow in your life?

You've got to pay a little attention to producing some fruit. But you don't do that by simply concentrating and trying harder. You do it by abiding in Christ. You do everything you can to draw closer to him. You soak yourself in his Word. You do your best to obey, to say yes to him. You respond to his discipline, trying to learn and grow instead of rebelling against the painful things that happen to you. And as you do this, your life will start producing the sweet, juicy, luscious fruit that makes life good for you and for others.

You'll grow more patient, in other words.

You'll be more loving, less concerned with having your own way.

You'll be more gentle, but at the same time more confident and determined to do what is right.

You'll have a better sense of what is important, what you can control, when you should act, when you should wait.

And right in the middle of all this fertile production, you'll discover the seeds of hope, all ready to sprout and grow.

Hope is the inevitable by-product
of the transformation
Jesus wants to make in our lives.

A Hopeful Hint

*Planting seeds or bulbs can be a won-
derful investment of hope. Plant a bed
of daffodil or tulip bulbs in the fall and
wait for their bright, hopeful faces in the
springtime.*

Words of Hope—
and Hope from
the Word

If seeds in the black earth can turn into such beautiful roses, what might not the heart of man become in its long journey toward the stars?

—G. K. Chesterton

But the fruit of the Spirit is love, joy, peace, patience, kindness, goodness, faithfulness, gentleness and self-control. Against such things there is no law....Since we live by the Spirit, let us keep in step with the Spirit.

—Galatians 5:22-25

Those of us who see the Father's hand in the harvest rejoice, our hearts filled with joy. But we rejoice even more in the spiritual harvest. Out of our broken lives God brings forth the fruit of his kingdom. Can you see it in your life? From your branches hang sweet fruit....Lessons learned. Changes made. Relationships healed. Hope restored. It is all his doing. That's why we mark it with celebration.

—Wayne Jacobson

By their fruit you will recognize them. Do people pick grapes from thornbushes, or figs from thistles? Likewise every good tree bears good fruit, but a bad tree bears bad fruit.

—Matthew 7:16-17

137

22

Praise Him, Praise Him

There are some things God asks us to do in our lives that go against our most basic instincts. They make us want to argue: "But Lord, did you really mean that?" Or "Well, all right…but really, Lord…"

We may not actually sigh or roll our eyes, but in our hearts we're doing exactly that. Or at least that's been true of me. We were willing to obey, but it just didn't feel right.

What kind of commandments am I talking about?

Loving our enemies is one. So is forgiving those who hurt us. Giving up our lives in order to find life—that's a real challenge.

And to me, one of the toughest things the Word of God directs us to do is to be thankful for our suffering. To praise God for the trials and tribulations that bring us pain.

That just doesn't seem natural. It *isn't* natural—that's the point! But it works. It really does. There have been so many times when I've finally sighed and rolled my eyes and muttered, "Well, all right, Lord…" and then given up a grudging "thank you" for something painful I was going through. And in the very act of praising and giving thanks I've found hope.

"Dear Lord, I thank you for the weariness I feel after the past few seminars."

"Dear Father, I praise you for this betrayal from someone I trusted."

"Father God, I praise you for my dad's alcoholism and the fact that I never really got to be a little girl."

I'm not sure I completely understand how all this works—except that the very act of praising God and giving thanks to him tends to get our focus off ourselves and onto God, who really can help us with our pain. It is a way of reminding ourselves that God is in charge of everything that happens, that God has a purpose for our lives, and that God even uses the difficulties we face to draw us closer to him.

For me, at least, this process of refocusing brings enormous relief and fresh infusions of hope. Maybe not right away—I've had my share of days when I was offering my halfhearted praise because I knew I should, but I certainly didn't *feel* either grateful or devoted. But even those grudging acts of obedience started nudging me around to the proper orientation, getting me in position to receive the hope he had for me.

And now that I've had some experience in receiving hope through the acts of praise and thanksgiving, I've begun to trust the process more. Praise comes to me more easily now, even in the midst of difficult days. Thanksgiving is a more natural response to whatever comes.

Yes, there are still days when my heart cries, "Oh, no—I just don't feel like praising anybody today." When I'm still rolling my eyes and stomping my feet as I grudgingly obey.

But God, in his great mercy, can take whatever we manage to give him and turn it into a great bounty. And so even from my grudging offerings of praise and thanksgiving I receive the hope I need to carry me through.

~

It works—even when it doesn't make sense.
Praise and thanksgiving open the door
to hope in our hearts.

A Hopeful Hint

I always find that making a joyful noise gives me a more hopeful feeling. So if you're feeling low, try opening up your mouth and singing your way into hope. If you're self-conscious about your voice, sing in the shower, or put on a CD and sing along. You might as well do a happy dance while you're at it.

Words of Hope—
and Hope from
the Word

The game was to just find something about everything to be glad about—no matter what 'twas.... You see, when you're hunting for the glad things, you sort of forget the other kind.

—Eleanor H. Porter, *Pollyanna*

Be joyful always; pray continually; give thanks in all circumstances, for this is God's will for you in Christ Jesus.

—1 Thessalonians 5:16-18

If anyone could tell you the shortest, surest way to all happiness and perfection, he must tell you to make it a rule to yourself to thank and praise God for everything that happens to you. For it is certain that whatever seeming calamity happens to you, if you thank and praise God for it, you turn it into a blessing.

—William Law

As I conscientiously praised God for what was hard to bear in my life, I discovered that praise for the good became spontaneous. I could not hold it back. Old theological questions receded into the background altogether. Slowly my whole being came more awake. The quality of my seeing was different. Ordinary things like trees, telephone lines, and tap water filled me with wonder. With a heightened awareness of the created order I also gained a degree of detachment from my body. It became easier to live with uncertainty and to take a long view of the future. I stopped giving undue significance to day-to-day symptoms. I was no longer so sure that I knew what was good and what was bad. Looking back on my life I saw that some things which had seemed so promising at the time later turned out to be disastrous, and some that had felt terrible had turned out to be good. In special moments it was even evident to me that pain and joy were all of a piece. They were separate, but one. Each was the bearer of the other.

—Elizabeth O'Connor

But as for me, I will always have hope;
  I will praise you more and more.
My mouth will tell of your righteousness,
  of your salvation all day long,
  though I know not its measure....
Your righteousness reaches to the skies,
  O God, you who have done great things.
  Who, O God, is like you?
Though you have made me see troubles,
  many and bitter, you will restore my life again;
from the depths of the earth you will again
  bring me up.
You will increase my honor and comfort me
  once again.

—Psalm 71:14,15,19-21

In the deserts of the heart
  Let the healing fountains start,
In the prison of his days
  Teach the free man how to praise.

—W. H. Auden

144

23

When You Have to Cry Out

*H*ave you ever thought that crying and complaining could be an act of hope?

In this era of "positive thinking," I think we sometimes lose track of that basic truth.

Yes, a positive attitude is important. Yes, we should try to look on the bright side. Yes, we'll feel more cheerful if we act more cheerful.

But sometimes the only truthful reaction to what is happening in our lives is to cry out in pain or anger. And God is above all a God of truth—so he doesn't want us to lock these honest reactions behind a wall of "positive" cheer.

Until we are honest with ourselves and God about our pain and discouragement, in fact, we may remain locked into that discouragement. We may remain frozen in a false cheerfulness, gritting our teeth and determined to "look on the bright side"—when everything still looks dark and gloomy to our inner eyes. We'll be pulling down the shades to hide the dark interior of our soul rather than pulling up the shades to let the sunshine in.

That's not what the Bible does, though. In fact, the Word of God is absolutely full of people who whined and complained and griped and wept. They accused God of not caring, of not managing the universe right. They sulked and wallowed in self-pity and basically told God to leave them alone.

And what did God do with these people? Sometimes he corrected them—the way he corrected Jonah. Sometimes he answered with a vision of his power and sovereignty—as he did with Job. But a lot of the time, he just listened until they had gotten all the anger and hurt off their chests and then come back around to the realization that God would indeed take care of them and everything would be all right.

So many psalms read exactly like that. They begin with a complaint or an outpouring of anger or fear. They don't hold back anything. But by the end of the psalm, they almost always calm down and return to a peaceful or joyful affirmation that God is God, and God is good.

I don't think it's an accident that all this crying and complaining is in the Bible. I think it's all there to remind us that we really can trust God with our pain—and even to give us a place to put our pain. We can be honest with God about our feelings. We can pour out our hearts to him, confide our most negative feelings to him. We can even tell God when we're angry with him.

And God will be able to handle it. He can handle all our negative feelings if we'll just bring them to him instead of turning away and trying to handle them ourselves. Even more, he will draw us into his own story of pain and suffering and sacrifice...and resurrection hope.

That, to me, is especially the message of the psalms, which have ministered to me so often in the past few years: If we trust him with our pain—and even our whining and complaining—he will be faithful to lead us through it all and into a new place of peace and hope.

With that in mind, here are a few ideas for "creative complaining" that can help you turn to God in honesty and trust:

- *Read psalms!* Try to see them as a pattern for being both honest and faithful to God. Use them for comfort and insight, but also as an outlet for your own feelings. When I'm going through a tough time, sometimes the psalms are the most helpful parts of the Bible. I even like to read them aloud, to let them give words to my own feelings.

- *Get a journal and pour out your feelings on paper.* But begin all your journal entries with "Dear God" to remind you to trust God with all that's within you. (If you're having trouble getting started, try copying a psalm or two.)

- *If you are musical, trying singing the blues to God.* Spirituals like "Sometimes I Feel Like a Motherless Child" can be especially helpful in carrying your sorrow to God.

- *Invite God along on a walk and pour out your troubles to him.* I find that the act of exercising sometimes helps me be more direct and honest with God—as well as helping with the stress and anxiety.

- *Ask a trusted friend if you can complain to her.* Confiding in someone about your sorrows can be a holy and liberating act. But choose your friend carefully, and don't overload her with your pain. If you are struggling with a lot of negative feelings, a pastor or counselor might be a more appropriate choice.

- *Don't forget to thank God and praise him.* Even if you don't feel very thankful or very much like praising, try to end your gripe sessions with words of praise and thanksgiving. At very least, you can thank God for listening!

~

God really can handle your pain
and give you hope. Trust him.

A Hopeful Hint

Writing your own psalm can be a great way of coping when you're feeling discouraged. Before you start, read through a bunch of psalms in the Bible. Then follow their pattern as you pour out your feelings to the Lord. Tell him what's happening, how it makes you feel. Tell God what you wish he would do! But then, as you write, let him bring you around to a statement of praise and trust—and end your psalm on that note. Here's the pattern to follow: "Lord, this is happening to me, and this is awful, and I feel this way....But you are my God, and you will work it all out. So I will praise you!"

Words of Hope— and Hope from the Word

It is in the bad moments of my life that I must choose to learn the opportunity that hides at its deepest center. When my inadequacies rise, rebelling against my carefully constructed external persona then—then—God can get my attention.

—Karen Mains

Hear my prayer, O LORD;
  let my cry for help come to you.
Do not hide your face from me
  when I am in distress.
Turn your ear to me;
  when I call, answer me quickly.
For my days vanish like smoke;
  my bones burn like glowing embers.
My heart is blighted and withered like grass;
  I forget to eat my food.

150

Because of my loud groaning
  I am reduced to skin and bones…
For I eat ashes as my food
  and mingle my drink with tears
because of your great wrath,
  for you have taken me up and thrown
  me aside…
Do not take me away, O my God, in the
    midst of my days;
  your years go on through all generations.
In the beginning you laid the foundations of the
    earth,
  and the heavens are the work of your hands.
They will perish, but you remain;
  they will all wear out like a garment…
But you remain the same,
    and your years will never end.

—Psalm 102:1-5,9,10,24-27

"Many good things are painful," Phyllis said: giving birth to a child, writing a poem, asking for forgiveness. Phyllis thought it a very bad sign that Americans were so afraid of pain that they thought the worst thing in the world was to suffer. She felt suffering had brought her back to God, back to a real understanding of what was important in the world....Some people would say she had lost touch with reality in order to protect herself against its pain. I think, rather, she had gotten in touch with reality in a way that few of us ever do, and had seen its beauty.

—Daniel Taylor

24

Better Than New

*H*ow do you find hope when you've run out of possibilities?

When you've tried everything you know to do and your life is still not working?

Maybe you're staring failure in the face—a business that's going under, a marriage that's unraveling. Maybe you've hit a dead end—the habits that have helped you handle your pain are just making things worse, and you don't know what else to try. Maybe you've gotten so tangled up in your own mistakes that you don't know what thread to pull. Or maybe you're growing older and you fear you're running out of time.

How do you find hope when you've run out of possibilities?

If your life looks anything like that—and you're willing to admit it—then you're in the best possible place for finding the hope God has for you.

That's because God tends to do his best work when we human beings have run out of options. For only then are we apt to stop meddling and *let* him work.

In our lives, we tend to be like semiskilled householders trying to deal with a plumbing leak problem. We plunge and we wrench and we pour and we flush. Sometimes we manage to patch things up. Often we end up making things worse. But then comes that moment when it flashes across our minds: We need a plumber! And only then will we be on the way to really getting things fixed.

Now, if you happen to be really good with plumbing, I apologize. But the point I'm trying to make is that often our best hope for fixing our messed-up lives is to give up on our "do it yourself" efforts and call in the Expert. We need to give up our stubborn independence, admit we've messed things up, and finally agree to do things his way.

And when we do that, God steps in and begins to work the miracles in our lives.

Sometimes he can repair the damage with a few twists of a wrench.

Sometimes he might have to rip out some pipes and replace some fixtures.

He may even decide he has to do a complete remodeling job—and the process won't be painless or easy. We may have to give up things we like. We may need to stop clinging to the stopgap measures we've come to trust. And we'll never get things back the way they were.

But what we will have, if we trust the Expert and do what he says, is a life that works. A life full of love and light and newness.

Not just good.

But better than new.

God loves to bring hope
into your most hopeless situations.

A Hopeful Hint

*Have you ever kept a prayer journal? If
not, try it for at least a month or two as
a concrete tool for building up hope even
in seemingly hopeless situations. Use an
expensive notebook or blank book. Record the
date and your prayer requests on the left-
hand pages. Then, as your prayers are
answered, begin to write out the results of
you prayers on the right-hand pages—across
from the corresponding requests. Dedicate a
part of your daily prayer time to reading over
these results as well as writing new prayers.
You'll be surprised how seeing the concrete
results will build up your hope and your willingness to turn your problems over to God.*

Words of Hope— and Hope from the Word

I will repay you for the years the locusts have eaten....

—Joel 2:25

One of the first and most important spiritual truths that I appropriated as a newly committed Christian was this: Satan is a liar (John 8:44)! I have found that many, if not most, of his lies are centered around this main theme: hopelessness. He will find a million different ways to try to convince us that it's useless to try anymore, that our situation is unredeemable and we might as well give it up! If we believe those lies, he has won. Thank God, I had Christian friends who taught me how to recognize this voice of hopelessness and how to fight back. I learned early in my Christian walk to confront the lies in my head, just as Jesus confronted the lies of Satan in the wilderness.

—Claire Cloninger

Therefore, if anyone is in Christ, he is a new creation; the old has gone, the new has come! All this is from God, who reconciled us to himself through Christ and gave us the ministry of reconciliation.

—2 Corinthians 5:17-18

It is possible to begin again. It is hard and we never do it perfectly, but it can be done....I must begin again on joy and happiness, on forgiveness and peace, on gratitude and patience.

—Andrew Greeley

See, I am doing a new thing!
  Now it springs up; do you not perceive it?
I am making a way in the desert
  and streams in the wasteland.

—Isaiah 43:19

If you asked me how God has revealed himself to me, I should reply, he reveals himself as Newness.

—Carlo Carretto

That is a very old apple tree, but the blossoms this year seem more beautiful than ever before. That old tree grows a little new wood each year, and I suppose it is out of the new wood that these blossoms come. Like the apple tree, I try to grow a little new wood each year.

—Henry Wadsworth Longfellow

Man is born broken. He lives by mending. And the grace of God is the glue.

—Eugene O'Neill

25

Are We There Yet?

Sometimes when we think we've run out of hope, what we've really run out of is patience!

The truth is, God's sense of time is different from ours, and that means that life here on earth can involve a lot of waiting.

We have to wait to see our prayers answered.

We have to wait for God's miracles to unfold.

We have to wait for life to get better, for God to keep his promises.

Sometimes, it seems, we have to wait a long, long time. And we hate it!

We're like children in the backseat of a car, unable to comprehend when we'll *really* get where we're going. And like children in a backseat, we grow restless and irritable. We may even start doubting whether God knows what he's doing at all—whether there's any reason to hope.

I know I feel that way sometimes, especially in recent days. Sometimes I look upon my disease and it seems so big and I have endured it so long that I become discouraged. I can hardly believe all this—the tumors, the fatigue, the baldness, the treatments—is actually happening to me. I want so much to be well and to just go back to my normal way of life. Having cancer is just plain inconvenient!

And of course I've felt that way many times before—and you have too. We just get tired of waiting for God to do his work in our lives.

But it's times like that when we have to remind ourselves once more who we are—and who the Parent is!

God is God, and he operates on his own time. He knows the end from the beginning, and he has a bigger plan in mind than just giving us what we want when we want it. As we wait, he's shaping us, teaching us (if we will learn), testing and refining us. He knows we're children, and he's actually working to grow us up! He wants to teach us to live in his time.

Sometimes I think he cuts things close on purpose, just to teach us to trust him. Surely you've had that experience! You've prayed and nothing seems to happen. You've trusted and time is running out. You're already making contingency plans—what am I going to do if God lets me down? And then, at the very last minute, things come together. The waiting pays off. The outcome is so much better than anything you could have done on your own. And you should realize you just have kept on trusting!

"God is an 11:59 God," a friend of a friend of mine likes to say, "and we keep on thinking it's 12:20 when it's really only 11:39. So we wait, fidgeting in the backseat, for God to do what he said he would."

Sometimes, too, we're just waiting for feelings of hope to return. Sometimes our discouragement is simply the result of living in mortal bodies and living in a fallen world. Sometimes it just gets us down, and our sense of hope just drains away.

Even when we know better, the feelings of despair and discouragement can get to us. Even when we're not ready to give up hope, we can *feel* hopeless. But often, if we give it time, the hope that lies deep within us will bubble back up again.

In the meantime, what should you do with your fidgety, hopeless feelings?

First, you can remind yourself that the feelings of hopelessness are temporary and your waiting won't last forever. Just putting things in perspective can help a lot. Reading the Bible or good Christian books can help you do that. So can talking to your pastor or a wise Christian friend.

And remember, you can actually draw hope from other people. If you put yourself in the company of positive people, you'll probably feel more hopeful. If you confess to being discouraged, someone will probably reach out to encourage you. If feelings of hopelessness persist for several weeks, it's probably a good idea to talk to a doctor or counselor.

In the meantime, one of the best strategies you can adopt is to pray, leaning on God and claiming his promises. You can tell God how tired you are of waiting and ask for His help in getting through the waiting period.

Don't be afraid to ask God for a sign that he's still working. Don't be afraid to ask him to send you an encourager. Remember, God wants you to grow, but he doesn't want you to give up. He will give you what you need to endure your waiting period and keep moving forward toward hope.

In the meantime, it helps to keep on doing what you know to do—take care of yourself physically, stay in the Word, try to maintain your important relationships.

Then, finally, when you have done all these things to move past a time of restlessness or hopelessness, you may simply have to endure.

Like a desert explorer caught in a sandstorm, you might need to simply curl up and cover your head, waiting for things to get better before you travel on.

Or, like the fidgety child in a backseat who has colored all her pictures and played all her games, you might need to finally let your head drop and take a nap.

But the good news is that no matter what you do—whether you're fidgeting or fussing or resting and waiting, the car is still on the road.

Your heavenly Daddy will keep his promises.

He'll get you where you need to be—and he'll be right on time.

~

Even when we have the fidgets,
God's work is worth the wait.

Words of Hope—
and Hope from
the Word

Be patient. When you feel lonely, stay with your loneliness. Avoid the temptation to let your fearful self run off. Let it teach you its wisdom; let it tell you that you can live instead of just surviving. Gradually you will become one, and you will find that Jesus is living in your heart and offering you all you need.

—Henri Nouwen

For a thousand years in your sight
  are like a day that has just gone by,
  or like a watch in the night....
Teach us to number our days aright,
  that we may gain a heart of wisdom.

—Psalm 90:4,12

Hope and patience are two sovereign remedies for all, the surest reposals, the softest cushions to lean on in adversity.

—Robert Burton

Be patient, then, brothers, until the Lord's coming. See how the farmer waits for the land to yield its valuable crop and how patient he is for the autumn and spring rains. You too, be patient and stand firm, because the Lord's coming is near.

—James 5:7-8

Patience gains all things.
Who has God wants nothing.
God alone suffices.

—St. Theresa of Avila

For our light and momentary troubles are achieving for us an eternal glory that far outweighs them all. So we fix our eyes not on what is seen, but on what is unseen. For what is seen is temporary, but what is unseen is eternal.

—2 Corinthians 4:17-18

Remember the former things, those of long ago;
  I am God, and there is no other;
  I am God, and there is none like me.
I make known the end from the beginning,
  from ancient times, what is still to come.
I say: My purpose will stand,
  and I will do all that I please....
What I have said, that will I bring about;
  what I have planned, that will I do.
Listen to me, you stubborn-hearted,
  you who are far from righteousness.
I am bringing my righteousness near,
  it is not far away;
  and my salvation will not be delayed.

—Isaiah 46:9-13

Peace does not dwell in outward things, but in
the heart prepared to wait trustfully and quietly
on him who has all things safely in his hands.

—Elisabeth Elliot

When our hopes break, let our patience hold.

—Thomas Fuller

26

Hope for Your Every Need

$\mathcal{P}$ractically speaking, I believe a lot of hopelessness comes from fear. Not fear of anything specific—but a deep, underlying, panicky fear that we won't get what we need—that what we are given won't be enough.

There are many reasons for this.

Perhaps we didn't get our needs met as a child, and this sense of neglect still lingers in our hearts.

Perhaps we haven't quite grown up, and we're expecting others to do for us what we need to learn to do for ourselves.

Perhaps we have this underlying sense that we're not worth taking care of or that we shouldn't need any help.

Or perhaps we have difficulty trusting that God really *is* sufficient to take care of what we need.

Whatever the reason, the fear and panic can build until our hope seems to disappear to the point that it's hard to muster any hope.

Even worse, the fear of not getting what we need can cause us *not* to get what we need. Perhaps we fail to give our bodies appropriate nutrition, exercise, and medical treatment. Or we cut ourselves off emotionally, depriving ourselves of the love and connection we need. We might even shut ourselves off from God, to the point that we can't sense his love and care. It's a painful cycle that leads to still more fear, panic, and discouragement.

How can we stop this needy cycle and build up our hope instead? Here are some ideas that have proved healing to me.

First, it's important to tell yourself the truth—which is that God loves you, that God cares for you, that God wants you to have what you need and will see that you get it. Tell that to yourself over and over. Read the Scriptures at the end of this chapter. Remind yourself that God made you the way you are. Because God is a loving Father, not a sadist, he wouldn't make you with needs that cannot be met.

(This doesn't mean that you'll always get what you want or that you should put your needs above those of others. Not at all! There's a big difference between accepting God's provision thankfully and insisting on your own way.)

Second, consider that you may be looking for gratification of your needs in all the wrong places. You may be expecting a person to give you the kind of security that only God can give. Or you may be expecting someone else to take care of things that you should be taking care of yourself.

Third, prayerfully consider whether you're getting in the way of having your needs met. Is there part of you that feels you don't deserve God's care? Are you holding on to guilt that you should confess to the Lord and get rid of? Are you still punishing yourself for something God has already forgiven you for? If any of these things are true, you might need to do a little work with a pastor or a counselor.

In the meantime, though, you can cut down on your fear and discouragement by nurturing yourself a little better and, in the process, opening your heart to feel God's care.

Start by trying a little more deliberately to give your body what it needs. Feed it healthy foods. Stretch it and pump it. Cut down on the stress you subject it to. Try to accept the fact that your body is part of God's gift of life. Say "thank you" by letting its needs be attended to.

You might pay a little extra attention to giving your soul what it needs, too. And what any soul needs most of all is quiet time with God. Just fifteen minutes a day can make a big difference. Spending time in the Word is another way to care for your soul's needs. So can making a point to spend time with positive people and with those you love. And try to make a little space for creative pursuits you find fulfilling—whether it is writing poetry, playing the flute, or planning a garden.

Most of all, try to open your heart and let God meet your needs. He's a loving Father, and he wants to hold you in his arms. He wants to nurture you, care for you, and help you grow.

He wants, more than anyone else in this entire world, to give you hope!

∼

It's the hopeful truth:
God wants to take care of you.
Let him.

Words of Hope— and Hope from the Word

Can a mother forget the baby at her breast and have no compassion on the child she has borne? Though she may forget, I will not forget you! See, I have engraved you on the palms of my hands.

—Isaiah 49:15-16

Cast all your anxiety on him because he cares for you.

—1 Peter 5:7

Keep your heart with all diligence, for out of it spring the issues of life.

—Proverbs 4:23 NKJV

Do not look forward to the changes and chances of this life in fear; rather look to them with full hope that, as they arise, God, whose you are, will deliver you out of them. He has kept you hitherto—do you but hold fast to his dear hand, and he will lead you safely through all things; and, when you cannot stand, he will bear you in his arms. Do not look forward to what may happen tomorrow; the same everlasting Father who cares for you today will take care of you tomorrow, and every day. Either he will shield you from suffering, or he will give you unfailing strength to bear it. Be at peace, then, and put aside all anxious thoughts and imaginations.

—Francis de Sales

27

Surrounded by Hope

*O*ne simple, practical way to increase the sense of hope in your life is to add a touch of hopefulness to your environment.

I don't mean you have to redecorate your house or spend a lot of money on new things. But just a little extra attention to your daily surroundings can make a big difference in how hopeful you feel.

Just pick a room where you spend a lot of your time—the kitchen, your office, even the master bathroom. Take a cup of tea into that room, sit quietly, and look around. Consider the color, the arrangement of furniture, even the basket of laundry in the corner.

Then think: What is there about the room that tends to make you feel hopeful, alive, energized, and ready to move forward? Do you love the pictures of family that cluster in a corner? The cheery light from the window? The gospel music playing on the radio?

And what is there about the room that drags down your spirits and tempts you to give up? Do the piles of work on your desk fill you with dread and a sense that you'll never get ahead? Do the dark drapes and upholstery depress you? Is there a table that keeps dinging your shins?

Then choose three changes you can make in that room to enhance its hopefulness as an environment.

The first change should be very simple—something you could get up from your chair and do right now—like straightening the piles of papers, putting away the scattered shoes on the floor, or putting a pretty cloth on the table.

The second should be a change you could make over a weekend—like rearranging the furniture, sewing new valances for the windows, or buying plants.

The third should be a longer-term plan—like repainting the room, setting up a file system, or revamping the way your family approaches chores.

Now, stop what you are doing and take care of item number one. You can probably do it in five minutes or less. Don't you feel more hopeful and energized already? You may be inspired to tackle a few more five-minute projects right away! But before you get carried away, take a little time to plan for items two and three, in that order.

Do you have a free weekend coming up in which you can tackle number two or bite off a big chunk of three? If not, break both projects up into as many components as you can. Resolve to work on them in fifteen- or thirty-minute increments until you have them done.

While you're working on your three steps to a more hopeful environment, you might want to put a little more thought into what tends to make you more hopeful. The questions below will serve as a helpful checklist for surrounding yourself with signs of hope. As you answer them, though, remember that different people will answer these questions different ways. I myself would answer them differently at various times of my life!

- *What kinds of colors tend to lift my spirits and make me more optimistic* (energetic brights, gentle pastels, nurturing earth tones, dignified darks)?

- *What kind of music makes me feel more energetic or peaceful* (soothing instrumentals, rousing praise, peppy pop)?

- *Do any particular fragrances inspire hopeful thoughts* (clean citrus, soft florals, spicy scents, baking bread)?

- *Are any visual symbols especially meaningful to me—either because of their beauty or symbolism* (a daffodil or narcissus, a rising sun, a cross, faces of children, landscapes)?

- *Do any particular Scriptures or quotations stick in my mind and inspire hope?*

- *What kind of housekeeping tends to make me feel hopeful* (easygoing, with works-in-progress ready at hand, books on tables, comfortable clutter—or clean, sparse, and simple)?

- *Do I own any special objects that makes me smile and encourage me* (a gift from a friend, a treasured book, a family heirloom, a silly memento)?

It should be obvious when you complete the list that surrounding yourself with hopeful colors, hopeful music, hopeful objects, even hopeful smells can help you build a more hopeful environment. In addition, the act of shaping your environment to set yourself up for hope can lift your spirits and set your heart to moving forward.

It can't create hope in a hopeless heart. (Hope, remember, comes from God.)

But it can help you replenish your hope when your cup drains a little low.

∾

When hope is all around you,
it's hard to ignore.

Words of Hope—
and Hope from
the Word

Worship the Lord *in the beauty of holiness.*

—Psalm 29:2 NKJV

*One's own surroundings mean so much to one,
when one is feeling miserable.*

—Edith Sitwell

*I am still confident of this:
I will see the goodness of the* Lord
*in the land of the living.
Wait for the* Lord;
*be strong and take heart
and wait for the* Lord.

—Psalm 27:13-14

Never lose an opportunity of seeing anything that is beautiful; for beauty is God's handwriting—a wayside sacrament. Welcome it in every fair face, in every fair sky, in every flower, and thank God for it as a cup of blessing.

—Ralph Waldo Emerson

I like to think of the word "living-rooms" being short for the joy-of-living rooms. That is what they ought to be—full of life and happiness and beauty [and hope].

—Lucy Abbot Throop

28

The Hope Underground

*H*ave you ever spent any time in an oncologist's office? Unfortunately, I've gotten to know that particular suite pretty well in the last two years. And when I first started to go, I thought it was the most dismal, depressing place—sort of like a clubhouse for the dying.

Well, now I have a completely different perspective on that office. I've come to think of it as a headquarters for the Hope Underground. It's full of people who encourage me by their example of courage and perseverance and self-giving love in the face of suffering. They're the ones who have called me, written me, brought me fresh strawberries from the farmer's market. They've given me tips about where to find wigs and suggested tricks for making my therapies easier. They've held my hand when I couldn't laugh and talked to me when I couldn't stand to be touched.

The doctors and nurses in my oncologist's office are also part of the Hope Underground. I've heard that I'm lucky in this—that not everyone's experience is this positive. But I'm grateful for the men and women who care for me so tenderly, paying attention to my emotional and spiritual needs as well as my physical ones. Some of the staff have even prayed with me.

And *I've* joined the Hope Underground, too—or at least I hope I have! We give to each other. We support each other. And this entire experience has taught me, more eloquently than ever, that one of the most important ways we can find hope is to bring hope to others. And one of the most hope-giving things we can do for others is to share in their suffering.

Does the idea of hope through suffering sound strange to you? It's another one of those truths that goes against the grain of our human instincts. We don't *want* to suffer. Nobody really wants to join the Hope Underground.

But the suffering is going to happen one way or another, whether we like it or not. You may not develop cancer, but you may have to live with a broken home. Or you may lose a child or be caught in a tornado or earthquake. I don't know exactly what will happen in the course of your lifetime, but I know that at one time or another you're going to face pain and suffering.

And when that happens, the only real choice is whether you're going to suffer alone or whether you're going to join the hopeful company of the Hope Underground.

Suffering, you see, can change you for the better—if you let it.

It can sharpen your focus on what is really important and what is merely extraneous. It can intensify your joy in the miracle of living. It can show you who your real friends are—and make those relationships sweeter.

If you let it, suffering can make you more patient, more trusting, more willing to wait for what is good. It can make you more loving, more tender, more understanding. It can make you more empathetic, more willing to give the gift of listening to and simply being with another.

Most important, suffering can bring you into closer fellowship with the crucified and risen Christ—for he is the founding member of the Hope Underground.

It was through his own suffering that he lived into undying hope.

Hope through suffering. It happens. I've seen it happen—and it happens most beautifully when the suffering is shared. So here's the question to ask when suffering engulfs you.

Are you just going to let it hurt?

Or will you let the hurt propel you into the loving, giving company of the Hope Underground?

~

Suffering can strengthen your hope
by drawing you close to Christ.

Shared suffering can sweeten your hope
by keeping you close to other people.

Words of Hope—
and Hope from
the Word

We rejoice in the hope of the glory of God. Not only so, but we also rejoice in our sufferings, because we know that suffering produces perseverance; perseverance, character; and character, hope. And hope does not disappoint us, because God has poured out his love into our hearts by the Holy Spirit, whom he has given us.

—Romans 5:2-5

I learned what it was to put yourself in someone else's place. I learned that by accepting limitations, you make life a richer experience. And I learned that people can be healed even if they are not cured.

—Cappy Capossela
(speaking of her own experience
with the Hope Underground)

At the point where men and women lose hope, where they become powerless and can do nothing more, the lonely, assailed and forsaken Christ waits for them and gives them a share in his passion....Our disappointments, our lonelinesses and our defeats do not separate us from him; they draw us more deeply into communion with him.

—Jürgen Moltmann

Dear friends, do not be surprised at the painful trial you are suffering, as though something strange were happening to you. But rejoice that you participate in the sufferings of Christ, so that you may be overjoyed when his glory is revealed.

—1 Peter 4:12-13

The disease which raged in my limbs and stole my energy also made me open to anything that might make me well, an attitude that is one of the primary gifts of pain. It unlocks our closed world.

—Elizabeth O'Connor

183

And the God of all grace, who called you to his eternal glory in Christ, after you have suffered a little while, will himself restore you and make you strong, firm, and steadfast. To him be the power for ever and ever.

—1 Peter 5:10-11

Jesus opened himself up entirely to the fear and suffering....He said, "If it is possible, let this cup pass from me," but he kept his eye on the prize, which was feeling loved by God, which is new life. And he let people he loved keep him company in his suffering, which is about as radical a concept as I can imagine. I don't want people's company when I have the flu or PMS. But when friends of mine have opened up to this willingness to have companionship at the end of their lives, or when they were losing or had lost a child, which may be the same thing, at some point they found themselves involved with material that enabled them to hook onto something bigger than the grasping, crying "I." They plugged in to all of life that surrounds us, that shimmers with loss and light and movement, the very broth of creation, the salty, the sweet, what's real.

—Anne Lamott

29

Getting Your Hopes Up

*D*on't get your hopes up!"

Did anyone ever say that to you as a child? Did you ever say it to a child?

That's the kind of thing people say to children to protect them from disappointment, from that crushing feeling of having your hopes dashed.

I *know* you know what that's like!

You hoped for a raise, for a new house, for a husband. You prayed. You waited. You trusted.

And it didn't happen.

There was no raise (or it wasn't big enough).

You didn't get the house (or the roof leaked).

You never found the right man (or the one you got drives you crazy!).

And you felt the same kind of disappointment you felt as a child when the hoped-for bicycle didn't arrive under the Christmas tree.

It hurts to get your hopes up and then be let down.

So is it better never to get your hopes up—just so you can avoid that kind of discouragement?

I don't think so!

Remember, we *need* hope. We need the motivation and energy and buoyancy it brings. There's a reason our eyes are in the front of our head—we're created to look forward to our life!

So what can we do to avoid the big letdown?

Well, it helps to give a little thought to what you're hoping for. Are they realistic, trustworthy things or merely pie in the sky? Are they based on your understanding of what God wants in your life, or is there an element of disobedience? Would you really *want* your hopes to become reality, or are they simply a pleasant diversion—a daydream? (There's nothing wrong with daydreams, but they're nothing to get our hopes up about.)

But I don't think we need to edit our hopes that closely. We don't need to limit our hopes only to what we can reasonably expect to come true. Doing that would take all the hopefulness out of our hope. It would close off our sense of possibility, of adventure, of delicious surprise.

No, I think what we need to do is not to suppress our hopes, but strengthen our trust. We need to keep our hopes high, knowing that God will help us handle our disappointments.

We can hope—literally—to our hearts' content, if we stay as close as possible to the Hope that will never leave us.

∾

It's really not hard to live in hope
when you know you can never really fall!

A Hopeful Hint

When you're tempted to say, "It's hope-less," practice saying instead, "I wonder what God's going to do next?" Just changing your words can help turn your heart around from despair to hope.

Words of Hope—
and Hope from
the Word

*Now faith is being sure of what we hope for
and certain of what we do not see. This is what
the ancients were commended for.*

—Hebrews 11:1-2

*When you say a situation or a person is hopeless,
you are slamming the door in the face of God.*

—Charles L. Allen

*Watch ye, watch ye
and be ready to meet me,
for lo, I come at noonday.
Fear ye not, fear ye not,
for with my hand I will lead you on,
and safely I'll guide your little boat
beyond this vale of sorrow.*

—Shaker hymn

Against all hope, Abraham in hope believed and so became the father of many nations, just as it had been said to him, "So shall your offspring be." Without weakening in his faith, he faced the fact that his body was as good as dead—since he was about a hundred years old—and that Sarah's womb was also dead. Yet he did not waver through unbelief regarding the promise of God, but was strengthened in his faith and gave glory to God, being fully persuaded that God had power to do what he had promised. This is why "it was credited to him as righteousness."

—Romans 4:18-22

He that lives in hope danceth without music.

—George Herbert

Let us hold unswervingly to the hope we profess, for he who promised is faithful.

—Hebrews 10:23

"May our Lord Jesus Christ himself and God our Father, who loved us and by his grace gave us eternal encouragement and good hope, encourage your hearts and strengthen you in every good deed and word" (2 Thessalonians 2:16-17).

Hugs—and Hope!

Emilie Barnes